SPOKE

PLANG PHO

ปลั่ง พลอยพรหม

รวมสาส์น

รวมหนังสือสำหรับทุกคนในครอบครัว

SPOKEN THAI
PLANG PHORYPHORHM

Fourth Edition 1996
ISBN 974-246-091-4

Published & Distributed By
RUAMSARN (1977) CO.,LTD.
864 Burabha Palace, Bangkok 10200.
Tel. 226-3808, 221-6483, Fax. 222-2036

พิมพ์ที่ อักษรพิทยา

61 ถนนมหรรณพ กทม. 10200

นายชูศักดิ์ หล่อสุวรรณศิริ ผู้พิมพ์ผู้โฆษณา

MAP OF BANGKOK METR

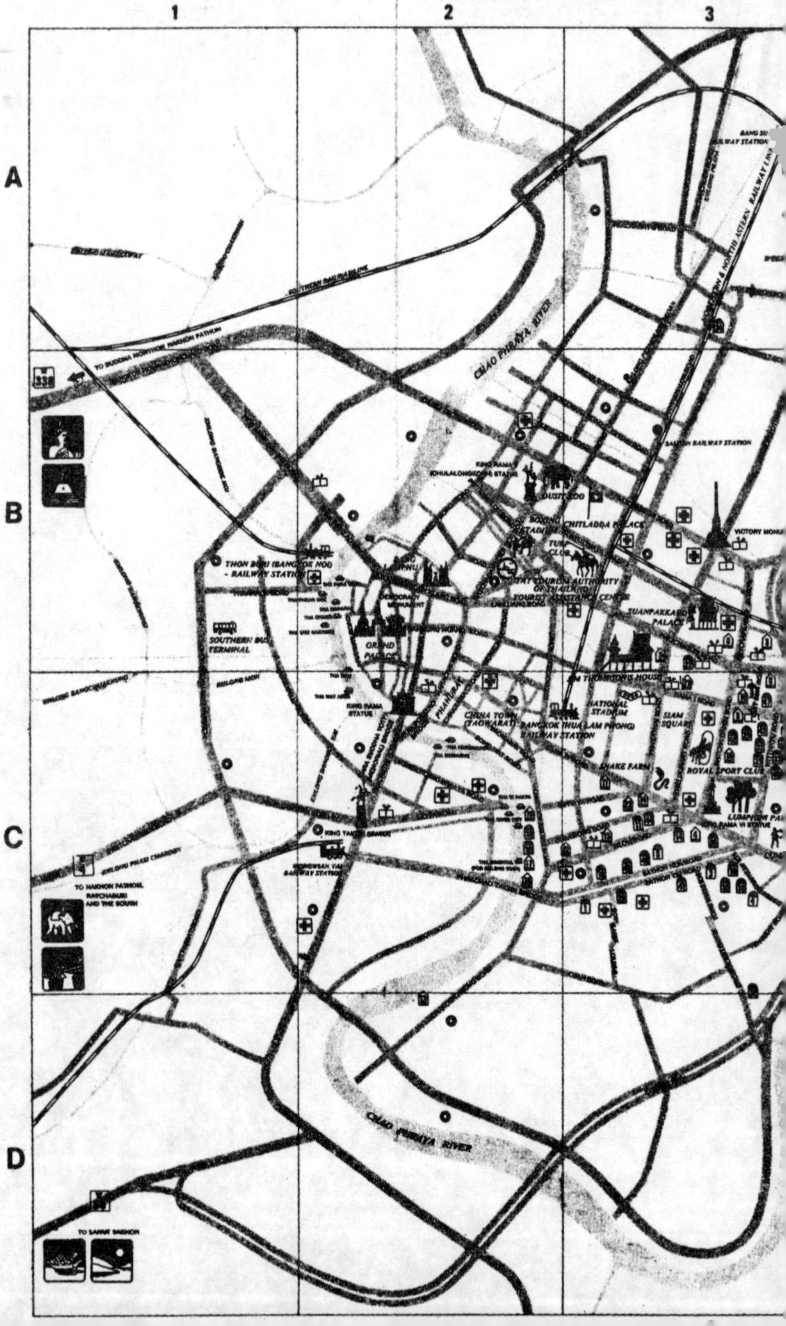

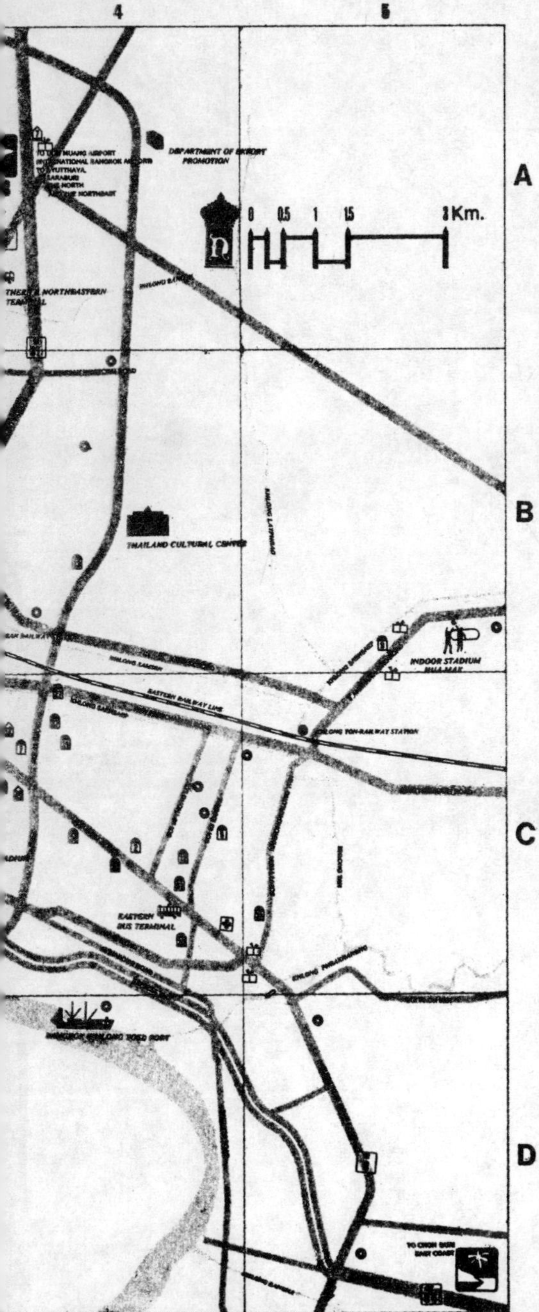

SYMBOL

- Hotel
- Ambassador
- Shopping Area
- Hospital
- Police Station
- Pier

HOTEL

1. Ambassador C4
2. Asia B3
3. Bangkok Palace B3
4. Dusit Thani C3
5. Erawan C3
6. Hilton International C3
7. Hyatt Central Plaza A4
8. Indra Regent B3
9. The Landmark C4
10. Le Meridian President C3
11. Mandarin C3
12. Manhattan C4
13. The Menam D2
14. Montien C3
15. Narai C3
16. New Imperial C3
17. The Oriental C2
18. The Regent Bangkok C3
19. Royal Orchid Sheraton C2
20. Shangrila C2
21. Siam Intercontinental C3
22. Silom Plaza C3
23. Tawana Ramada C3
24. Windzor C4

AMBASSADOR

1. Apostolic Nuncieture C3
2. Argentina C4
3. Australia C3
4. Austria C3
5. Bangladesh C4
6. Belgium C3
7. Brazil C4
8. Brunei C3
9. Bulgaria B5
10. Burma C3
11. Canada C3
12. Chile C4
13. China B4
14. Czechoslovakia C3
15. Denmark C3
16. Egypt C3
17. Finland C3
18. France C2
19. Germany C3
20. Hungary C4
21. India C4
22. Indonesia C3
23. Iran C3
24. Iraq A3
25. Israel C3
26. Italy D3
27. Japan C4
28. Korea C3
29. Laos C3
30. Malaysia C3
31. Nepal C5
32. The Netherlands C3
33. New Zealand C3
34. Norway C4
35. Pakistan C4
36. The Philippines C4
37. Poland C4
38. Portugal C2
39. Romania C4
40. Saudi Arabia C3
41. Singapore C3
42. Spain C3
43. Sri Lanka C3
44. Sweden C3
45. Switzerland C3
46. Turkey C3
47. United Kingdom C3
48. U.S.A. C3
49. U.S.S.R. C3
50. Vietnam C3
51. Yugoslavia C4

Foreword

Spoken Thai is prepared to help foreign visitors to Thailand who like to speak Thai. This small book contains lists of Thai consonants and vowels, Thai words and conversation. They would be of great use for our foreign visitors to practice speaking Thai and make their stay in Thailand as enjoyable as possible. We also hope it would help promoting better understanding international goodwill friendship between Thai people and our friends abroad.

Thai Phonetics and Systems

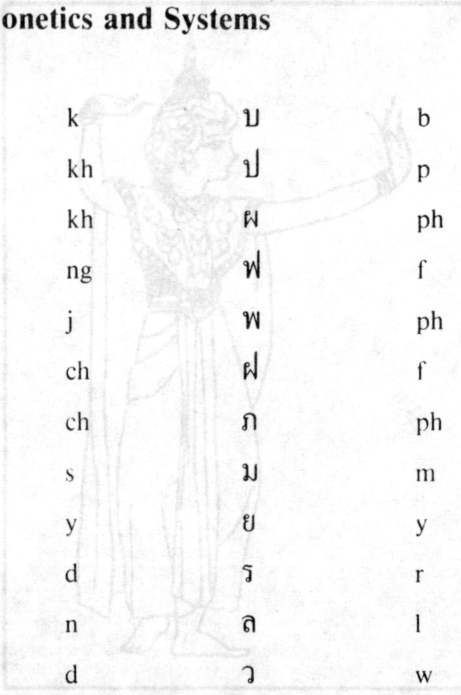

ก	k	บ	b
ข	kh	ป	p
ค	kh	ผ	ph
ง	ng	ฝ	f
จ	j	พ	ph
ฉ	ch	ฟ	f
ช	ch	ภ	ph
ซ	s	ม	m
ญ	y	ย	y
ฎ	d	ร	r
ณ	n	ล	l
ด	d	ว	w
ต	t	ศ	s
ถ	th	ษ	s
ท	th	ส	s
ธ	th	ห	h
น	n	ฬ	l
		อ	-
		ฮ	h

อะ	a	อา	a
อิ	i	อี	ee
อึ	oe	อือ	oe
อุ	u	อู	oo
เอะ	e	เอ	e
แอะ	ae	แอ	ae
โอะ	o	โอ	o
เอาะ	or	ออ	or
เออะ	er	เออ	er
เอียะ	ia	เอีย	ia
เอือะ	oea	เอือ	oea
อัวะ	ua	อัว	ua
อำ	am	เอย	oei
ใอ, ไอ	ai	อวย	uai
ออย	oi	โอย	oiy
เอา	ao	อิว	iu
อุย	ui		

Pronunciation Guide

อยู่ในใบแทรก

NOTE

1. Long or stressed vowels are underlined.
2. Normal tone : not marked
3. ·· low tone (เสียงเอก) ··
4. / falling tone (เสียงโท) \
5. V high tone (เสียงตรี) ^
6. / rising tone (เสียงจัตวา) /

Pronunciation

Consonants

k as in kin- กิน

(to eat), is similar to "g" in "gun"

kh as in khit- คิด

(to think)

ng as in ngai̇ ง่าย

(easy), is like "ng" in "singer"

J as in jai- ใจ

(heart), is like "j" in "Jim"

ch as in chuai̇ ช่วย

(help)

s as in sa̱m สาม

(three), is like "s" in "see"

y as in yäi- ใหญ่

(big), is like "y" in "your"

d as in dee- ดี

(good), is like "d" in "day"

t as in ta ตา

(eye), is like "t" in "stand"

th as in Thai ไทย

(Thai)

n as in neè นี่

(this), is like "n" in "non"

b as in bàn บ้าน

(home), is like "b" in "boy"

p as in pai ไป

(to go)

f as in fan ฟัน

(tooth) is like "f" in "food"

m as in mee มี

(there is), is like "m" in "milk"

r as in rân ร้าน

(a shop)

l as in ท loeàk เลือก

(to choose), is like "l" in "loud"

w as in wan วัน

(a day), is like "w" in "way"

Vowels

a as in käp กับ

- (with), is short-like "u" in "cup"

a̲ as in thá̲m ถาม

- (to ask), is long like "a" in "car"

ae as in khaéng แข็ง

(hard), is similar to "a" in "lang"

a̲e̲ as in khäek แขก

(a guest), is the long version of the same sound "ae"

e as in hén เห็น

(to see), is short like "e" in "men"

e̲ as in phle̲ng เพลง

(a song), is the long version of the same sound "e"

i as in pïd ปิด

(to close), is like "i" in "sit"

ee as in pee ปี

(year), is like "ee" in "see"

o as in khon คน

- khon (a person), is a short rounded "o"

o as in nòn โน่น

(over there), is like "o" in "stone"

or as in ข khoŕ ขอ

(please), is like "a" in "saw" (not pronounce "r")

oe as in thoéng ถึง

(to arrive)

oe as in loem ลืม

(to forget), is the long version of "oe"

er as in ngern เงิน

- (money), not pronounce "r"

u as in khun คุณ

- (you), is the "u" in "put"

oo as in jöop จูบ

- (to kiss), is like "oo" in "wood"

Dipthongs and Vowel Clusters

ai as in khäi ไข่

(an egg), is the short version of the sound "ai"

ai as in khaí ขาย

(to sell) is like "y" in "my"

ao as in phaó เผา

(to burn),

ia as in mìa เมีย

- (a wife), (i) is more stressed and a little longer than (a)

iao as in khiáó เขียว

- (green), (i) is more stressed than (o , and (o) is little more stressed than (a)

iu as in hiú หิว

- (to be hungry), (i) is more stressed and a little more longer than (u)

oiy as in doiy โดย

- (with), (o) is longer and more stressed than (i)

oi as in khoi คอย

- (to wait), is like "oy" in "toy"

oea as in moeá เมื่อ

- (when), oe is more stressed and a little longer than (a)

oei as in khoei เคย

- (to be used to), (oe) is longer and more stressed than (i)

ua as in khuad ขวด

(a bottle), (u) is more stressed and a little longer than (a)

uai as in ruai รวย

(to be rich), (u) is more stressed and a little longer than (a) and (i)

Use of Thai Pronouns

There are lots of Pronouns in Thai language; even Pronouns of the same person differ according to the persons spoken to and the speakers themselves.

I, me	Chán (to friends and people in general, but-not-to elders or people of high rank)		ฉัน
	phóm (male)	to high ranking	ผม
	di̇̇-chán (female)	people	ดิฉัน
We, us	rao, phuàk rao (male and female)		เรา, พวกเรา
	phuàk-phóm (male)		พวกผม
	phuàk-di̇-chán (female)		พวกดิฉัน
you	thạ̀n	high ranking	ท่าน
	khun	person	คุณ
	ther (to friends and low ranking person)		เธอ
he, him she, her	khaó		เขา
they, them	Khaó thâng-laí		เขาทั้งหลาย

Thai Names

We have first names and second names or surnames, and we are called by our first names. The word "nai" is used before the names of men, and "Nang sao" is used before the names of women; the names of boys and girls under fifteen years of age are titled "Dĕk-chai" and "Dĕk-yíng" respectively.

After being married, the wife's second name is changed into that of the husband, and the word "Nang" is put before her name instead "of" "Nang-sao".

e.g.	Nai-sa-man-Ma-dee
	Nang-sao-see-sa-morn-Ma-dee
	Dek-chai-sa-mai-Ma-dee
	Dek-ying-see-sai-Ma-dee
Ma-dee	is the second name or surname
	Mrs.-see-sa-morn-Pra-sert
Pra-sert	is Mrs. see-sa-morn's second name after her marriage

20 Relations

relations	yàt-phèe-nôrng	ญาติพี่น้อง
family	khròrb-khrua	ครอบครัว
parents	phòr-maè	พ่อแม่

father	phòr̲	พ่อ
mother	maè̲	แม่
child children	loòk	ลูก
daughter	loòk-saó	ลูกสาว
son	loòk-chai	ลูกชาย
husband	sá̲-mee, phuá	สามี, ผัว
wife	phan-ra-ya̲, mia	ภรรยา, เมีย
boy	dëk-chai	เด็กชาย
girl	dëk-yíng	เด็กหญิง
man, men	phoò-chai	ผู้ชาย
woman, women	phoò-yíng	ผู้หญิง

grand father		
- mother's father	ta̲	ตา
- father's father	pöo	ปู่

grand mother		
- mother's mother	yai	ยาย
- father's mother	yà̲	ย่า
great-grand father great-grand mother	tuàd	ทวด

uncle		
- elder brothers of father or mother	lung	ลุง
- younger brother or sister of father	a̲	อา
- younger brother or sister of mother	nâ̲	น้า
aunt		
- elder sister of mother	pà̲	ป้า

nephew	lá̲n-chai i	หลานชาย
niece	lá̲n-sao	หลานสาว
grand nephew grand niece	lé̲̲n	เหลน
younger brother	nô̲r̲ng-chai	น้องชาย
younger sister	nô̲r̲ng-sáo	น้องสาว
elder brother	pheè-chai	พี่ชาย
elder sister	pheè-sáo	พี่สาว
relatives	yà̲t	ญาติ
close relatives	yà̲t-sa-nït t	ญาติสนิท

How is your family ?

khrorb-khrua-khun-sä-bai-dee-roé?

ครอบครัวคุณสบายดีหรือ ?

How are your parents ?

phòr-maè-khun-sä-bai-dee-roé?

พ่อแม่คุณสบายดีหรือ ?

Fine, thank you.

sä-bai-dee-khòrb-khun.

สบายดี ขอบคุณ.

Are your parents still living ?

phòr-maè-khun-yang-yöo-roé?

พ่อแม่คุณยังอยู่หรือ ?

Yes, they are.

yang-yöo.

ยังอยู่.

Have you any brothers or sisters ?

khun-mee-pheè-nôrng-maí?

คุณมีพี่น้องไหม ?

I have two younger sisters.

chán-mee-nôrng-sao-sorńg-khon.

ฉันมีน้องสาวสองคน

How many brothers have you ?

khun-mee-pheè-chai-nôrng-chai-këe-knon?

คุณมีพี่ชายน้องชายกี่คน ?

I have one elder brother.

chán-mee-pheè-chai-nöeng-khon.

ฉันมีพี่ชายหนึ่งคน.

How old is your brother ?

pheè-chai-khun-a-yû-thaò-rai?

พี่ชายคุณอายุเท่าไร ?

Twenty years old.

yeè-sib-pee.

ยี่สิบปี.

I have a few relations.

chán-mee-yàt-sorng-sám-khon.

ฉันมีญาติสองสามคน.

Parts of the Body

arm	khaén	แขน
ankle	khor̀-thaô	ข้อเท้า
adam's apple	loòk-kra-doëak	ลูกกระเดือก
body	ràng-kai	ร่างกาย
brain	sä-morńg	สมอง
back	láng	หลัง
back bone	kra-dook-sán-láng	กระดูกสันหลัง
blood	loeàd	เลือด

beard	khrao	เครา
bone	kra-dook	กระดูก
bladder	kra-phôr-pat-sä-wâ	กระเพาะปัสสาวะ
cheek	kaèm	แก้ม
chin	khang	คาง
clavicle	hai-pla-râ	ไหปลาร้า
calf	nòng	น่อง
chest	suang-ök	ทรวงอก
complenion	phíu-phan	ผิวพรรณ
eye	ta	ตา
eye-brow	khîu	คิ้ว
eye-lash	khón-ta	ขนตา
elbow	khoȉ-soȉk	ข้อศอก
face	nà	หน้า
forehead	nà-phäk	หน้าผาก
finger	nîu-moe	นิ้วมือ
finger nail	lêb-moe	เล็บมือ
foot, feet	thâo	เท้า
gum	ngoëak	เหงือก
head	seé-sä, húa	ศีรษะ, หัว
hair	phóm	ผม
hand	moe	มือ

hip	sä-phòk	สะโพก
heep	sòn-thao	ส้นเท้า
heart	huá-jai	หัวใจ
knee	khäo	เข่า
lip	lim-feé-pàk	ริมฝีปาก
lung	pörd	ปอด
liver	täb	ตับ
mouth	pàk	ปาก
moustache	nüat	หนวด
muscle	klàm-neôa	กล้ามเนื้อ
mind	jit-jai	จิตใจ
nose	ja-möok	จมูก
neck	khor	คอ
nerve	pra-sät	ประสาท
palm	fä-moe :	ฝ่ามือ
rib	seè-khrong	ซี่โครง
shoulder	läi	ไหล่
skin	phíu-náng	ผิวหนัง
spleen	mâm	ม้าม
stomach	thôrng	ท้อง
tooth, teeth	fan	ฟัน
tongue	lîn	ลิ้น
throat	lam-khor	ลำคอ

tendon	en	เอ็น
toe nail	lêb-thâo	เล็บเท้า
voice	siang	เสียง
wrist	khoȓ-moe	ข้อมือ

Everyday Movement

everyday	thûk-wan	ทุกวัน
movement	kan-khloeàn-waí	การเคลื่อนไหว
to move	khloeàn-wai	เคลื่อนไหว
to sit	nàng	นั่ง
to lie down	norn	นอน
to lie on one's back	norn-ngaí	นอนหงาย
to lie on one's stomach	norn-kwam̀	นอนคว่ำ
to lie on one's side	norn-tä-khaeng	นอนตะแคง
to sleep	norn-läb	นอนหลับ
to wake up to get up	töen-norn	ตื่นนอน
to sleep like a log	norn-läb-pen-tai	นอนหลับ เป็นตาย
to stand	yoen	ยืน
to walk	dern	เดิน
to jump, to leap	kra-död	กระโดด
to take a bath	äb-nâm	อาบน้ำ
to soap one's body	thoó-tua-duaì-sa-böo	ถูตัวด้วยสบู่
to wash one's face	lâng-nà	ล้างหน้า
to brush one's tooth	seé-fan	สีฟัน
to clean one's mouth	buàn-päk	บ้วนปาก
to wash one's hand	lâng-moe	ล้างมือ
to dry one's body	chêd-tua	เช็ดตัว

to powder one's face	phäd-na̲	ผัดหน้า
to comb one's hair	weé-phóm	หวีผม
to get-dressed	taëng-tua	แต่งตัว
get dressed	taëng-tua-siá	แต่งตัวเสีย
to put on one's shirt		
to put on one's blouse	suám-soea	สวมเสื้อ
to put-on one's dress	su̲ám-soe̲à̲ -kra-pro̲ng	สวมเสื้อ กระโปรง
to put one's coat	su̲ám-so̲è̲a̲-no̲rk	สวมเสื้อนอก
to put on one's skirt	nùng-kra-pro̲ng	นุ่งกระโปรง
to put on one's socks	su̲ám-thúng-thaô	สวมถุงเท้า
to put on one's shoes	su̲ám-ro̲rng-thaô	สวมรองเท้า
to kick	të	เตะ
to box	töi	ต่อย
to eat	kin	กิน
to chew	khî̲ao	เคี้ยว
to swallow	kl̲oe̲n	กลืน
to drink	doèm-nâ̲m	ดื่มน้ำ
to smoke	söob-bu-rëe	สูบบุหรี่
to say, to speak	phòod	พูด
to converse, to chat	khui, són-thâna̲	คุย, สนทนา

to laugh	huá-rôr	หัวเราะ
to smile	yîm	ยิ้ม
to cry	rôrng-haì	ร้องไห้
to sob	sä-oèn	สะอื้น
to cough	ai	ไอ
to yawn	haó-norn	หาวนอน
to whistle	phîu-päk	ผิวปาก
to write	khián	เขียน
to read	än	อ่าน
to whisper	kra-sîb	กระซิบ
to sing	rorng-pleng	ร้องเพลง
to push	phlàk-dan	ผลักดัน
to draw	làk	ลาก
to pull	doeng	ดึง
to beat	tee	ตี
to scold	du, dä	ดุ, ด่า
to throw	khwàng, paa	ขว้าง, ปา

I am sleepy
chan-nguàng-norn
ฉันง่วงนอน

Did you stay up late last night?
moeà-khoen-khun-norn-döek-roé?
เมื่อคืนคุณนอนดึกหรือ ?

I went out with my friend.
chán-ork-pai-käb-phoeàn
ฉันออกไปกับเพื่อน.

I got up early this morning.
moeà-châo-chán-töen-täe-châo.
เมื่อเช้าฉันตื่นแต่เช้า.

Is anybody crying ?
khrai-rôrng-haì-roé ?
ใครร้องไห้หรือ ?

My son is hungry.
loòk-chai-chán-hiú.
ลูกชายฉันหิว.

They are laughing.
kháo-kam-lang-huá-rôr.
เขากำลังหัวเราะ.

Do you smoke ?
khun-söob-bu-reè-maí ?
คุณสูบบุหรี่ไหม ?

I am writing to my mother.
chán-kam-lang-khián-thoéng-maè.
ฉันกำลังเขียนถึงแม่.

To whom do you speak ?
khun-phöod-kub-khrai ?
คุณพูดกับใคร ?

My sister sings very well.

nôrng-saó-chán-rôrng-phleng-dee-màk.

น้องสาวฉันร้องเพลงดีมาก.

He likes to take exercise.

kháo-chorb-ork-kam-lang-kai.

เขาชอบออกกำลังกาย.

The Day of the Week

1 มกราคม 2533 JANUARY 1990

อาทิตย์ SUN	จันทร์ MON	อังคาร TUE	พุธ WED	พฤหัฯ THU	ศุกร์ FRI	เสาร์ SAT
●	1 ขึ้น 6 ค่ำ เดือน 2	2 ขึ้น 7 ค่ำ	3 ◑ ขึ้น 8 ค่ำ	4 ขึ้น 9 ค่ำ	5 ขึ้น 10 ค่ำ	6 ขึ้น 11 ค่ำ
7 ขึ้น 12 ค่ำ	8 ขึ้น 13 ค่ำ	9 ขึ้น 14 ค่ำ	10 ○ ขึ้น 15 ค่ำ	11 แรม 1 ค่ำ	12 แรม 2 ค่ำ	13 แรม 3 ค่ำ

Day	wan	วัน
week	süb-da̱	สัปดาห์
Sunday	wan-a̱-thi̇̂t	วันอาทิตย์
Monday	wan-jan	วันจันทร์
Tuesday	wan-ang-kha̱n	วันอังคาร
Wednesday	wan-phût	วันพุธ
Thursday	wan-phâ-roe-hät	วันพฤหัส
Friday	wan-sük	วันศุกร์
Saturday	wan-saó	วันเสาร์

What is today ?
wan-nêe-wan-ä-rai ?
วันนี้วันอะไร ?
It's Thursday.
wan-phâ-roe-hät.
วันพฤหัส.

What was yesterday ?

moeà-wan-wan-a-rai ?

เมื่อวานวันอะไร ?

It was Wednesday.

wan-phût.

วันพุธ.

What is tomorrow ?

phrùng-nêe-wan-a-rai ?

พรุ่งนี้วันอะไร ?

When will he come ?

khao-ja-ma-moeà-rai ?

เขาจะมาเมื่อไร ?

He will come on Sunday.

kháo-ja-ma wan-a -thît.

เขาจะมาวันอาทิตย์.

When did you come back ?

khun-klab-ma-moeà-rai ?

คุณกลับมาเมื่อไร ?

I came back on Monday.

chán-klab-ma-moeà-wan-jan.

ฉันกลับมาเมื่อวันจันทร์.

Did you see him on Thursday ?

khun-phôb-khaó-moeà-wan-ang-khan-roé ?

คุณพบเขาเมื่อวันอังคารหรือ ?

36

The Months of the Year.

month	doean	เดือน
year	pee	ปี
January	doean-mok-ka-ra-khom	เดือนมกราคม
February	doean-kum-pha-phan	เดือนกุมภาพันธ์
March	doean-mee-na-khom	เดือนมีนาคม
April	doean-me-sa-yon	เดือนเมษายน
May	doean-phôed-sa-pha-khom	เดือนพฤษภาคม
June	doean-mi-thü-na-yon	เดือนมิถุนายน
July	doean-ka-râk-ka-da-khom	เดือนกรกฎาคม
August	doean-sińg-há-khom	เดือนสิงหาคม
September	doean-kan-ya-yon	เดือนกันยายน
October	doean-tu-la-khom	เดือนตุลาคม
November	doean-phroed-sä-ji-ka-yon	เดือนพฤศจิกายน
December	doean-than-wa-khom.	เดือนธันวาคม

What is this month ?

doean-nêe-doean-ä-rai ?

เดือนนี้เดือนอะไร ?

It's December.

doean-than-wa-khom

เดือนธันวาคม.

What is the first month of the year ?

doean-ä-rai-pen-doean-raèk-khorńg-pee ?

เดือนอะไรเป็นเดือนแรกของปี ?

It's January.

doean-mok-ka-ra-khom.

เดือนมกราคม.

What is the last month of the year ?

doean-ä-rai-pen-doean-sud-thaî-khorńg-pee ?

เดือนอะไรเป็นเดือนสุดท้ายของปี ?

When did you come ?

khun-ma-moeà-rai ?

คุณมาเมื่อไร ?

I came in April.

chán-ma-moea-doean-me-sá-yon.

ฉันมาเมื่อเดือนเมษายน.

What month is summer ?

doean-ä-rai-pen-rôe-doo-rôrn ?

เดือนอะไรเป็นฤดูร้อน ?

It's April.

doean-me-sa-yon.

เดือนเมษายน.

What month do you like best ?

khun-chorb-doean-ä-rai-màk-theè-süd ?

คุณชอบเดือนอะไรมากที่สุด ?

The Season of the Year.

season	rôe-doo	ฤดู

There are three seasons in Thailand.

Winter	rôe-doo-naó	ฤดูหนาว
(October to January)		
Summer	rôe-doo-rôrn	ฤดูร้อน
(February to April)		
Rainy Season	rôe-doo-fón	ฤดูฝน

It's very hot in Summer
nai-rôe-doo-rôrn-a-kat-rôrn-màk.
ในฤดูร้อนอากาศร้อนมาก.

It's not very cold in winter.
nai-rôe-doo-naó-a-kat-mài-naó-mak.
ในฤดูหนาวอากาศไม่หนาวมาก.

Winter may be very short in some years.
bang-pee-rôe-doo-naó-sân-mak.
บางปีฤดูหนาวสั้นมาก.

It's very wet in the rainy season.
fón-tok-màk-nai-rôe-doo-fón.
ฝนตกมากในฤดูฝน.

I don't like rainy season.
chán-mai-chorb-rôe-doo-fón.
ฉันไม่ชอบฤดูฝน.

The Time of a Day.

Time	we-la	เวลา
Day	wan	วัน
Today	wan-nêe	วันนี้
Tomorrow	phrung-nêe	พรุ่งนี้
Yesterday	moeà-warn-nêe	เมื่อวานนี้

The day after tomorrow.
ma-roen-nêe.
มะรืนนี้.

The day before yesterday.
wan-soen-nêe.
วานซืนนี้.

at night.
we-la-klang-khoen.
เวลากลางคืน.

in the daytime.
we-la-klang-wan.
เวลากลางวัน.

in the morning	we-la-châo	เวลาเช้า
in the after noon	we-la-bai	เวลาบ่าย
in the evening	we-la-yen	เวลาเย็น
at noon	we-la-thiàng	เวลาเที่ยง
at present,	we-la-nêe	เวลานี้
now	khä-na-nêe	ขณะนี้
nowadays	thûk-wan-nêe	ทุกวันนี้
late	sai	สาย
late at night	döek	ดึก
everyday	thûk-wan	ทุกวัน
every other day	wan-wên-wan	วันเว้นวัน

every two days	thûk-wan	ทุกสองวัน
every year	thûk-pee	ทุกปี
every night	thûk-khoen	ทุกคืน
every Sunday	thûk-wan-a-thit	ทุกวันอาทิตย์
every hour	thûk-chua-mong	ทุกชั่วโมง
every week	thûk-säb-da	ทุกสัปดาห์
day and night	thâng-wan-thâng-khoen	ทั้งวันทั้งคืน
at all times	thûk-we-la	ทุกเวลา
at that time	nai-we-la-nân	ในเวลานั้น
at night long	ta-lort-khoen	ตลอดคืน
all day long	ta-lort-wan	ตลอดวัน
recently	moeà-rew-rew-nêe	เมื่อเร็ว ๆ นี้
just now	moeà-ta-kêe-nêe:	เมื่อตะกี้นี้
in the future	nai-a-na-khôt	ในอนาคต
next year	pee-nà	ปีหน้า
next month	doean-nà	เดือนหน้า
last year	pee-theè-lâew	ปีที่แล้ว
last month	doean-theè-lâew	เดือนที่แล้ว
soon, not long	nai-mai-châ	ในไม่ช้า
when	moeà-rai	เมื่อไร

When will he come ?

khao-ja-ma-moeà-rai ?

เขาจะมาเมื่อไร ?

When will you go ?
khun-ja-pai-moeà-rai ?
คุณจะไปเมื่อไร ?

When will you do this ?
khun-ja-tham-roeàng-nêe-moeà-rai ?
คุณจะทำเรื่องนี้เมื่อไร ?

Please give me time.
khoŕ-we-la-chán-säk-nöi.
ขอเวลาฉันสักหน่อย.

In a few days.
eek-soŕng-sám-wan.
อีก 2-3 วัน.

right now	diaú-nêe	เดี๋ยวนี้
1 a.m.	jet-mong-châo	เจ็ดโมงเช้า
3 p.m.	bäi-sám-mong	บ่ายสามโมง
12 a.m.	thiàng	เที่ยง
12 p.m.	thiàng-khoen	เที่ยงคืน
half-past one	jet-mong-khroèng	เจ็ดโมงครึ่ง
or	bai-mong-khroèng	บ่ายโมงครึ่ง
a quarter past one	jet-mong-sib-hà -na-thee	เจ็ดโมงสิบห้า นาที
or	bai-mong- -sib-ha-na-thee	บ่ายโมง สิบห้านาที

a quarter to one	ëek-sib-ha-na-thee-ja-bäi-mong	อีกสิบห้านาทีจะบ่ายโมง

Excuse me, can you tell me the time ?
khor-thod-këe-mong-laêw ?
ขอโทษกี่โมงแล้ว ?

What's the time ?
What time is it now ?
What time do you have ?

këe-mong-laêw ?	กี่โมงแล้ว
we-la-thaò-rai-laêw ?	เวลาเท่าไรแล้ว

It's nine o'clock.
It's just nine o'clock.

kaò-mong	เก้าโมง

It's exactly nine o'clock.
It's nine o'clock sharp.

kao-mong-trong	เก้าโมงตรง

It's nine ten.
It's ten after nine.

kao-mong-sib-na-thee	เก้าโมงสิบนาที

It's a quarter after ten.

sib-mong-sib-hà-na-thee	สิบโมงห้าสิบนาที

It's half past ten

sib-mong-khroèng	สิบโมงครึ่ง

It's ten to eight.

ëek-sib-na-thee-ja-päed-mong	อีกสิบนาทีจะแปดโมง

Before ten o'clock.

körn-sib-mong ก่อนสิบโมง

after seven o'clock.

láng-jet-mong หลังเจ็ดโมง

punctual	trong-we-la	ตรงเวลา
It's late	sai-lâew, châ-pai i	สายแล้ว, ช้าไป
It's still early.	yang-châo-yöo	ยังเช้าอยู่
on time	trong-we-la	ตรงเวลา
in time	than-we-la	ทันเวลา

Is the plane on time ?

khroeàng-bin-throng-we-la-maí ?

เครื่องบินตรงเวลาไหม ?

Ten minutes late.

châ-pai-sib-na-thee

ช้าไปสิบนาที.

Shall we be in time ?

rao-ja-than-we-la-maí ?

เราจะทันเวลาไหม ?

Time of arrival.

we-la-ma-thoéng

เวลามาถึง.

Time of departure.

we-la-örk.

เวลาออก.

Time's up.	möd-we-la-lâew	หมดเวลาแล้ว
It's time to leave.	toéng-we-la-pai-lâew	ถึงเวลาไปแล้ว
It's time to go to bed.	toéng-we-la- -norn-lâew	ถึงเวลา นอนแล้ว
It will soon be dark.	ja-mòed-lâew	จะมืดแล้ว
It's late at night.	döek-lâew	ดึกแล้ว
Bangkok time	we-la -krung-thèp	เวลากรุงเทพฯ
Standard time	we-la-màt-tra-thán	เวลามาตรฐาน
I saw her yesterday	chán-phôb-khaó- -moèa-warn-nêe	ฉันพบเขา - เมื่อวานนี้
- last Sunday	-moèa-wan- -a-thit-kôrn	- เมื่อวัน อาทิตย์ก่อน
- last night	-moèa-khoen-nêe	- เมื่อคืนนี้
I shall see him	chán-ja-phob-khaó o	ฉันจะพบเขา
- tomorrow	-prùng-nêe	- พรุ่งนี้
- to night	-khoen-nêe	- คืนนี้
- this evening	-yen-nêe	- เย็นนี้
- next month	-doean-nà	- เดือนหน้า

I'm leaving	chán-ja-pai	ฉันจะไป
- to night	-khoen-nêe	- คืนนี้
- tomorrow	-phrung-nêe	- พรุ่งนี้
- next Monday	-wan-jan-nà	- วันจันทร์หน้า
I'm sorry,	khoŕ-thòt	ขอโทษ
- I'm late	-chan-ma-châ-pai	- ฉันมาช้าไป
- I'm too early	-chan-ma-rew-pai	- ฉันมาเร็วไป
- I've lost my money	-chan-tham -ngern-haí i	- ฉันทำ เงินหาย
I'll meet you tomorrow	chán-ja-pai-pôb -khun-prùng-nêe	ฉันจะไปพบ คุณพรุ่งนี้
Shall we meet at night ?	rao-ja-phob-kan -khlang-khoen -daì-maí ?	เราจะพบกัน กลางคืน ได้ไหม ?

A watch

watch	na-r̂i-ka	นาฬิกา
I have set my watch.	chán-tàng-na -r̂i-ka-lâew	ฉันตั้งนาฬิกาแล้ว
The watch is fast.	na-ri-ka-rew-pai i	นาฬิกาเร็วไป
The watch is slow.	na-ri-ka-châ-pai ai	นาฬิกาช้าไป
The watch has stopped.	na-ri-ka-taï	นาฬิกาตาย
The watch is out of order.	na-ri-ka-siá	นาฬิกาเสีย
The watch is run down.	na-ri-ka-möd -lan-lâew	นาฬิกาหมดลานแล้ว
Three minutes slow.	châ-pai-sám -na-thee	ช้าไป 3 นาที
Five minutes fast.	rew-pai-hà-na-thee	เร็วไปห้านาที
Please wind up the watch.	chuai-khaí-lan- -haì-duaì	ช่วยไขลานให้ด้วย
My watch keeps good time.	na-ri-ka-khóng- -chán-dern-trong	นาฬิกาของ ฉันเดินตรง
I want a strap for my watch.	chán-tòng-kan- -sai-na-ri-ka	ฉันต้องการ สายนาฬิกา
I want to have my watch repaired.	chán-tòng-kan- -kaè-na-ri-ka	ฉันต้องการ แก้นาฬิกา
When is it finished ?	söd-moeà-raï ?	เสร็จเมื่อไร ?

Counting

to count	nâb	นับ
counting	ka-nâb	การนับ

Cardinal Number

1	noêng	หนึ่ง
2	sórng	สอง
3	sám	สาม
4	sëe	สี่
5	hà	ห้า
6	hök	หก
7	jëd	เจ็ด
8	pâed	แปด
9	kaò	เก้า
10	sïb	สิบ
11	sïb-ëd	สิบเอ็ด
12	sïb-sórng	สิบสอง
13	sïb-sám	สิบสาม
14	sïb-sëe	สิบสี่
15	sïb-hà	สิบห้า
16	sïb-hök	สิบหก
17	sïb-jëd	สิบเจ็ด
18	sïb-pâed	สิบแปด
19	sïb-kào	สิบเก้า
20	yeè-sïb	ยี่สิบ
21	yeè-sïb-ëd	ยี่สิบเอ็ด
22	yeè-sïb-sórng	ยี่สิบสอง
23	yeè-sïb-sám	ยี่สิบสาม

28	yeè-sïb-pâed	ยี่สิบแปด
29	yeè-sïb-kàò	ยี่สิบเก้า
30	sám -sïb	สามสิบ
31	sám-sïb-ëd	สามสิบเอ็ด
32	sám-sïb-soŕng	สามสิบสอง
34	sám-sïb-sëë	สามสิบสี่
38	sám-sïb-pâed	สามสิบแปด
40	seė-sïb	สี่สิบ
41	seë-sïb-ëd	สี่สิบเอ็ด
42	seë-sïb-soŕng	สี่สิบสอง
45	seë-sïb-hà	สี่สิบห้า
49	seë-sïb-kào	สี่สิบเก้า
50	hà -sïb	ห้าสิบ
51	hà-sïb-ëd	ห้าสิบเอ็ด
59	hà-sïb-kào	ห้าสิบเก้า
60	hök-sïb	หกสิบ
62	hök-sïb-soŕng	หกสิบสอง
68	hök-sïb-pâed	หกสิบแปด
70	jed-sïb	เจ็ดสิบ
71	jëd-sïb-ëd	เจ็ดสิบเอ็ด
79	jëd-sïb-kào	เจ็ดสิบเก้า
80	pâed-sïb	แปดสิบ
90	kào-sïb	เก้าสิบ

92	kào-sïb-só̲rng	เก้าสิบสอง
96	kào-sïb-hök	เก้าสิบหก
100	noëng-rôi	หนึ่งร้อย
101	noëng-rôi-noëng	หนึ่งร้อยหนึ่ง
102	noëng-rôi-só̲rng	หนึ่งร้อยสอง
109	noëng-rôi-kào	หนึ่งร้อยเก้า
110	noëng-rôi-sïb	หนึ่งร้อยสิบ
120	noëng-rôi-yèe-sïb	หนึ่งร้อยยี่สิบ
121	noëng-rôi-yèe-sïb-ëd	หนึ่งร้อยยี่สิบเอ็ด
129	noëng-rôi-yèe-sïb-kào	หนึ่งร้อยยี่สิบเก้า
130	noëng-rôi-sám-sïb	หนึ่งร้อยสามสิบ
140	noëng-rôi-seë-sïb	หนึ่งร้อยสี่สิบ
150	noëng-rôi-hàr-sïb	หนึ่งร้อยห้าสิบ
160	noëng-rôi-hök-sïb	หนึ่งร้อยหกสิบ
190	noëng-rôi-kào-sïb	หนึ่งร้อยเก้าสิบ
200	só̲rng-rôi	สองร้อย
300	sá̲m-rôi	สามร้อย
400	seë-rôi	สี่ร้อย
900	kào-rôi	เก้าร้อย
910	kaô-rôi-sïb	เก้าร้อยสิบ
920	kaò-rôi-yèe-sïb	เก้าร้อยยี่สิบ
990	kaò-rôi-kào-sïb	เก้าร้อยเก้าสิบ
999	kaò-rôi-kào-sïb-kaò	เก้าร้อยเก้าสิบเก้า

1,000	noëng-phan	หนึ่งพัน
1,100	noëng-phan-noëng-rôi	หนึ่งพันหนึ่งร้อย
1,200	noëng-phan-sórng-rôi	หนึ่งพันสองร้อย
1,250	noëng-phan-sórng-rôi-hà-sïb	หนึ่งพันสองร้อยห้าสิบ
1,300	noëng-phan-sám-rôi	หนึ่งพันสามร้อย
1,400	noëng-phan-sëë-rôi	หนึ่งพันสี่ร้อย
1,450	noëng-phan-sëë-rôi-hà-sïb	หนึ่งพันสี่ร้อยห้าสิบ
1,500	noëng-phan-hà-rôi	หนึ่งพันห้าร้อย
1,600	noëng-phan-hök-rôi	หนึ่งพันหกร้อย
1,800	noëng-phan-pâed-rôi	หนึ่งพันแปดร้อย
2,000	sórng-phan	สองพัน
2,500	sórng-phan-hà-rôi	สองพันห้าร้อย
3,000	sám-phan	สามพัน
4,600	seë-phan-hök-rôi	สี่พันหกร้อย
4,700	seë-phan-jëd-rôi	สี่พันเจ็ดร้อย
8,000	pâed-phan	แปดพัน
9,000	kào-phan	เก้าพัน
9,500	kào-phan-hà-rôi	เก้าพันห้าร้อย
10,000	noëng-möen	หนึ่งหมื่น
15,000	noëng-möen-hà-phan	หนึ่งหมื่นห้าพัน
100,000	noëng-saén	หนึ่งแสน
150,000	noëng-saén-hà-möen	หนึ่งแสนห้าหมื่น
1,000,000	noëng-lân	หนึ่งล้าน

Ordinal Number

In Thai language, cardinal numbers can be changed into ordinal numbers by adding the word "tee" before the cardinal numbers.

1st	theè-noëng	ที่หนึ่ง
2nd	theè-só̲rng	ที่สอง
3rd	theè-sá̲m	ที่สาม
4th	theè-seë	ที่สี่
5th	theè-hà̲	ที่ห้า
6th	theè-hök	ที่หก
7th	theè-jëd	ที่เจ็ด
8th	theè-pâ̲e̲d	ที่แปด
9th	theè-kào	ที่เก้า
10th	theè-sïb	ที่สิบ

11th	theè-sïb-ëd	ที่สิบเอ็ด
12th	theè-sïb-só̲rng	ที่สิบสอง
13th	theè-sïb-sá̲m	ที่สิบสาม
14th	theè-sïb-sëë	ที่สิบสี่
19th	theè-sïb-kào	ที่สิบเก้า
20th	theè-yèe-sïb	ที่ยี่สิบ
30th	theè-sá̲m-sïb	ที่สามสิบ
50th	thee-hà̲-sïb	ที่ห้าสิบ
100th	theè-noëng-rôi	ที่หนึ่งร้อย
150th	theè-noëng-rôi-hà̲-sïb	ที่หนึ่งร้อยห้าสิบ
200th	theè-só̲rng-rôi	ที่สองร้อย

Can you count ?
khun-nâb-pen-maí ?
คุณนับเป็นไหม ?
No, I can't.
Chan-nâb-maì-pen.
ฉันนับไม่เป็น.
Try to count them, will you ?
long-nâb-doo-ŝi ?
ลองนับดูซิ ?
How many can you count ?
khun-nâb-dai-thaò-rai ?
คุณนับได้เท่าไร ?

I can count ten.

chán-nâb-daì-toeńg-sïb.

ฉันนับได้ถึงสิบ.

There are twenty students.

mee-nak-rian-yee-sib-khon.

มีนักเรียนยี่สิบคน.

He is the first in the class.

khao-daì-theè-noëng-nai-chân.

เขาได้ที่หนึ่งในชั้น.

How old are you ?

khun-a-yu-thaò-rai ?

คุณอายุเท่าไร ?

seven-teen.

sib-jed.

สิบเจ็ด

When were you born ?

khun-kërd-moeà-rai ?

คุณเกิดเมื่อไร ?

July 15th, 2510.

wan-theè-sïb-hà-ka-râk-ka-da-khom-sórng-phan-hà-rôi-sïb

วันที่ 15 กรกฎาคม พ.ศ. 2510.

Colours

colour	seé	สี
white	seé-khaó	สีขาว
red	seé-daeng	สีแดง
black	seé-dam	สีดำ
green	seé-khiaó	สีเขียว
yellow	seé-loeáng	สีเหลือง
blue	seé-nâm-ngern	สีน้ำเงิน
brown	seé-nâm-tan	สีน้ำตาล
orange	seé-sòm	สีส้ม
vermillion	seé-saëd	สีแสด
purple	seé-muàng	สีม่วง
golden	seé-thorng	สีทอง
grey	seé-thao	สีเทา
pink	seé-chom-phoo	สีชมพู
cream colour	seé-nuan	สีนวล
dark colour	seé-käe	สีแก่
light colour	seé-orn̈	สีอ่อน
dark blue	seé-nam-ngern-käe	สีน้ำเงินแก่
light grey	seé-thao-orn̈	สีเทาอ่อน
bright colour	seé-söd	สีสด
bright red	seé-daeng-söd	สีแดงสด
indigo	seé-khram	สีคราม

What colour is that ?

nàn-seé-a-rai ?

นั่นสีอะไร ?

It's pink.

seé-chom-phoo.

สีชมพู.

What colour do you like ?

khun-chorb-seé-a-rai ?

คุณชอบสีอะไร ?

I like light green.

chan-chor̈b-seé-khiaó-or̈n.

ฉันชอบสีเขียวอ่อน.

What colour is your skirt ?

kra-prong-khun-seé-a-rai ?

กระโปรงคุณสีอะไร ?

Greeting and Introducing

greeting	ka̲n-thâk-thai	การทักทาย
introducing	ka̲n-nâe-nam	การแนะนำ
good morning		
- afternoon	sa-wäd-dee	สวัสดี
- evening		
- day		

How do you do ?
sa-wad-dee ?
สวัสดี

How are you ?
sa-bai-dee-róe ?
สบายดีหรือ ?

Very well, thank you, and you ?
sa-bai-dee-khorb-khun-khun-la ?
สบายดีขอบคุณ, คุณล่ะ ?

Fine, thank you.
sa-bai-dee-khorb-khun.
สบายดีขอบคุณ.

I am glad to see you.
chan-yin-dee-theè-daì-pob-khun.
ฉันยินดีที่ได้พบคุณ.

Do you remember me ?
khun-jam-chán-daì-maí ?
คุณจำฉันได้ไหม ?

Yes, I do.
jam-daì.
จำได้.

I'm sorry, I don't.
khór-thòd-jam-mài-daì.
ขอโทษ จำไม่ได้.

Do you remember my name ?
khun-jam-choè-phóm-dài-mái ?
คุณจำชื่อผมได้ไหม ?

How is your family ?
khrob-khrua-khun-sä-bai-dee-roé ?
ครอบครัวคุณสบายดีหรือ ?

How is your wife ?
phan-ra-ya-khun-sä-bai-dee-roé ?
ภรรยาคุณสบายดีหรือ ?

Fine, thank you.
sa-bai-dee-khörb-khun.
สบายดี ขอบคุณ

How are the children ?
dek-dek-pen-yäng-rai ?
เด็ก ๆ เป็นอย่างไร ?

I haven't seen you for a long time.
phóm-maì-dàì-phôb-khun-siá-nan.
ผมไม่ได้พบคุณเสียนาน.

Do you like the weather today ?
khun-chorb-a-kät-wan-nêe-maí ?
คุณชอบอากาศวันนี้ไหม ?

Very hot indeed. I don't like it.
rôrn-màk-phóm-maì-chorb.
ร้อนมาก ผมไม่ชอบ.

May I introduce myself ? My name is Sombat.
phóm-khor-nâe-nam-tua-eng-phom-choè-som-bat.
ผมขอแนะนำตัวเอง ผมชื่อสมบัติ.

I am John.
phóm-choè-jorn.
ผมชื่อจอห์น.
I'm glad to meet you.
phóm-dee-jai-theè-daì-phob-khun.
ผมดีใจที่ได้พบคุณ.
How do you do ?
sä-wad-dee.
สวัสดี.
May I introduce Khun San to you ?
phóm-khór-nâe-nam-khun-sán-haì-rôo-jak-kab-khun.
ผมขอแนะนำคุณสันต์ให้รู้จักกับคุณ
Mr. San is a writer.
khun-Sán-pen-nâk-khián.
คุณสันต์เป็นนักเขียน.
I've heard much about you.
phóm-khoei-daì-yin-chòe-khun-ma-màk-lâew
ผมเคยได้ยินชื่อคุณมามากแล้ว.
Have you ever met Somsri ?
khun-khoei-phob-sóm-srí-maí ?
คุณเคยพบสมศรีไหม ?
I don't think we have met before.
chán-maì-khit-wà-rao-khoei-phob-kan-ma-körn
ฉันไม่คิดว่าเราเคยพบกันมาก่อน.

May I take you home ?

Allow me to take you home.

phóm-pha-khun-pai-söng-bàn-nâ

ผมพาคุณไปส่งบ้านนะ.

I should be delighted.

chán-yin-dee.

ฉันยินดี.

No, thank you.

maì-tòng-khörb-khun.

ไม่ต้องขอบคุณ

Won't you come in, please.

Come in, please.

chern-khaò-ma-nai-bàn.

เชิญเข้ามาในบ้าน .

Won't you sit down.

Take a seat.

chern-nàng.

เชิญนั่ง.

Best wishes to your family.

khor-söng-kwam-präd-thä-ná-dee-thoéng-khroŕb-khrua-khońg-khun.

ขอส่งความปรารถนาดีถึงครอบครัวของคุณ.

good night	ra-tree-sä-wät	ราตรีสวัสดิ์
good bye,	sä-wät-dee,	สวัสดี,

so long la-körn ลาก่อน

very nice to see you.
yin-dee-theë-daì-phôb-khun.
ยินดีที่ได้พบคุณ.
See you again.
laêw phôb-kan-ëek.
แล้วพบกันอีก.

Expressing Thanks

Thank you. khörb-khun ขอบคุณ
Thanks

Thank you for your kindness.
khörb-khun-sám-räb-kwam-ka-ru-na-khoŕng-khun.
ขอบคุณสำหรับความกรุณาของคุณ.

Thank you very much.
It's very kind of you.
khörb-khun-màk.
ขอบคุณมาก.

not at all.
It's a pleasure.
Don't mention it.
You're welcome.
Maì-pen-rai ไม่เป็นไร

Thank you just the same.
khörb-khun-khun-moeán-kan.
ขอบคุณคุณเหมือนกัน.

I am most grateful.
khörb-khun-màk
ขอบคุณมาก

excuses apologies	khoŕ-thòd	ขอโทษ
I am sorry. excuse me, please, excuse me.	khoŕ-thòd	ขอโทษ

Excuse me for being late.
khoŕ-thòd-theè-ma-saí.
ขอโทษที่มาสาย.

I'm terribly sorry.

I'm awfully sorry.

khoŕ-thòd-phóm-siá-jai-màk.

ขอโทษผมเสียใจมาก.

I beg your pardon.

Pardon me.

Please accept my apologies.

Do forgive me.

Forgive me, please.

phom-khoŕ-thòd.

ผมขอโทษ

Sorry to keep you waiting.

Khoŕ-thòd-theè-tham-hai-khung-tòng-khoi

ขอโทษที่ทำให้คุณต้องคอย.

I must apologize for disturbing you.

phom-khoŕ-thòd-theè-tòng-rôb-kuan-khun.

ผมขอโทษที่ต้องรบกวนคุณ.

That's all right.

It does not matter.

Don't worry about it at all.

mäi-pen-rai

ไม่เป็นไร.

Expressing Regrets

express	sä-daeng	แสดง
expressing	kan-sä-daeng	การแสดง
Regrets	kwaw-siá-jai	ความเสียใจ

I am sorry for you.
siá-jai-duaì.
เสียใจด้วย.

Please accept my sympathy.
Pröd-rab-kham-hén-jai-khoŕng-phóm.
โปรดรับความเห็นใจของผม.

Sorry, it's too late.
siá-jai-saí-kern-pai.
เสียใจสายเกินไป.

Sorry, I was out.
siá-jai-theè-phom-mai-yöo.
เสียใจที่ผมไม่อยู่.

Sorry, he was not in.
siá-jai-khao-mai-yöo.
เสียใจเขาไม่อยู่.

Sorry, I can't help you.
siá-jai-chan-chuai-khun-maì-daì.
เสียใจฉันช่วยคุณไม่ได้.

Sorry, we have to leave now.
siá-jai-rao-tong-pai-diáw-nêe-lâew.
เสียใจเราต้องไปเดี๋ยวนี้แล้ว.

Telephone-Mail-Callers.

Can you call me number.......... ?

chuaì-tör-maí-lḛk..........haì-theè

ช่วยต่อหมายเลข..........ให้ที.

Did anyone call me ?

mee-khrai-tho-thoéng-chán-maí ?

มีใครโทรฯ ถึงฉันไหม ?

Is there any mail for me ?

mee-jöd-maí-thoéng-chán-maí ?

มีจดหมายถึงฉันไหม ?

Have you any stamp ?

mee-sa-t̲a̲e̲m-maí ?

มีแสตมป์ไหม ?

Would you mail this for me, please ?

chuaì-thîng-jod-maí-haì-theè

ช่วยทิ้งจดหมายให้ที.

Are there any messages for me ?

mee-jod-maí-thoéng-chán-maí ?

มีจดหมายถึงฉันไหม ?

May I speak to Bob, please

khọ̲́r̲-phoòd-kab-bôb

ขอพูดกับบ๊อบ

Who's speaking, please ?

khrai-phoòd ?

ใครพูด ?

Just a moment, plaese.
pro̲d-kho̲i̲-sak-khroò.
โปรดคอยสักครู่.
There's a telephone call for you.
mee-tho̲-ra-sab-thoéng-khun.
มีโทรศัพท์ถึงคุณ.
Bob is speaking.
bôb-phoòd.
บ๊อบพูด.
Is Sang in ?
sa̲é̲ng-yöo-maí ?
แสงอยู่ไหม ?
No, he is out.
khaó-maì-yöo.
เขาไม่อยู่.
I'll call him back.
chán-ja-tho-klab-ma̲-ëëk
ฉันจะโทรกลับมาอีก
Can I leave a message for him ?
chán-säng-wâi-daì-maí ?
ฉันสั่งไว้ได้ไหม ?
Hold on, please.
yôk-hoó-wâi-kö̲r̲n.
ยกหูไว้ก่อน.

Feliz Navidad y Próspero Año
Battle of Hastings 1066
HAPPINESS
CHRISTMAS
POSTES POSTAGE
MERRY CHRISTMAS AND A HAPPY NEW YEAR
REPUBLIQUE FRANCAISE
CATHEDRALE DE SENS
FROHE WEIHNAC
Christmas
JOYEUX NOËL ET BONNE ANNÉE

ประเทศไทย THAILAND
POSTAGE
ชามฝา เบญจรงค์
COVERED BOWLS, BENCHARONG WARE
2.75 บาท BAHT
HELVETIA 20
1815-1965 VALAIS NEUCHÂTEL
FRIEDEN
PAX IN TERRA
POSTE VATICANE L.20
BUNDESPOST
God Jul och Gott Nytt År
Prettige Kerstdagen en Gelukkig Nieuwjaar

Don't replace the receiver.
yä-wang-hoó.
อย่าวางหู.

The line is engaged.
saí-maì-wa̠ng.
สายไม่ว่าง.

There's no reply.
maì-mee-siáng-tö̠rb.
ไม่มีเสียงตอบ.

I think you got the wrong number.
chán-khî̂t-wà̠-khun-dài-maí-lèk-phit
ฉันคิดว่าคุณได้หมายเลขผิด.

Could you tell me how much the call cost ?
khit-khà̠-tho̠-ra-sab-thào-räi.
คิดค่าโทรศัพท์เท่าไร ?

Dail the police station.
mún-pai-ro̠ng-phâk.
หมุนไปโรงพัก.

What number ?
maí-lè̠k-thaó-raí ?
หมายเลขเท่าไร ?

The line is out of order.
tho̠-ra-sab-siá.
โทรศัพท์เสีย.

Eating and Drinking

There are many types of eating and drinking places in Thailand.

Bar : Drinks and snacks are served. Most bars have hostesses whose drinks you have to pay.

Beer garden : Beer and snack are served.

Coffee shop : Coffee, solf drinks and snacks are served.

Resteaurant : Thai and western-style food are served.

eating	ka n-kin	การกิน
drinking	ka n-doem	การดื่ม

I'm hungry now.
chán-hiú-lâew.
ฉันหิวแล้ว.
I'm terribly thirsty.
chán-kra-hai-nâm-loeá-kern.
ฉันกระหายน้ำเหลือเกิน.
I want a coke.
chán yäk-daì-côk.
ฉันอยากได้โค้ก.
I want coffee badly.
chán yäk-döem-ka-fae-loeá-kern.
ฉันอยากดื่มกาแฟเหลือเกิน.

I don't like cold drinks.
chán-maì-chòrb-khroèang-döem-yen-yen.
ฉันไม่ชอบเครื่องดื่มเย็น ๆ

I like good food.
chán-chòrb-a-hán-dee-dee.
ฉันชอบอาหารดี ๆ

Menu, please.
khoŕ-rai-kan-a-hán.
ขอรายการอาหาร.

Give me this, please. (pointing)
khoŕ-yang-nêe.
ขออย่างนี้.

Do you need bread or rice with it ?
khun-tòrng-kan-kha-nóm-pang-roé-khàw-duaì-maí ?
คุณต้องการขนมปังหรือข้าวด้วยไหม ?

What shall I serve for drink ?
tòrng-kan-khroeàng-döem-a-rai ?
ต้องการเครื่องดื่มอะไร ?

Will you give me tea ?
khoŕ-cha.
ขอชา.

Same with me.
chán-khoŕ-moeán-kan.
ฉันขอเหมือนกัน.

What is this ?
neè-a-rai ?
นี่อะไร ?

How do you eat this ?
neè-kin-ya̱ng-rai ?
นี่กินอย่างไร ?

This is fine for me.
chán-cho̱r̀b-ya̱ng-nê̂e-la̱ê̂w
ฉันชอบอย่างนี้แล้ว.

I've never eaten this before.
chán-mai-khoei-kin-yän̈g-nê̂e-ma̱r-kö̱rn.
ฉันไม่เคยกินอย่างนี้มาก่อน.

I cannot eat pork.
chán-kin-moó-maì-daì.
ฉันกินหมูไม่ได้.

This is delicious. I love it.
neè-a-ròi-dee-chàn-cho̱r̀b.
นี่อร่อยดีฉันชอบ.

I have enough.
chán-pho̱r-laê̂w
ฉันพอแล้ว.

Thank you very much.
khorb-khun-mâ̱k
ขอบคุณมาก.

I'm reserved a table for four people.

chán-jorng-tô-sám-räb-séé-khon-wâi.

ฉันจองโต๊ะสำหรับ 4 คนไว้.

Please bring me the menu.

khor-rai-kan-a-hán.

ขอรายการอาหาร.

How do you like your meat done ?

khun-chorb-hài-tham-noêa-yäng-rai ?

คุณชอบให้ทำเนื้ออย่างไร ?

well done.

tham-hài-sük.

ทำให้สุก.

rare.

mai-torng-suk-nâk.

ไม่ต้องสุกนัก.

This is not what I order.

chán-mai-dài-säng-yäng-nêe.

ฉันไม่ได้สั่งอย่างนี้.

Can I have the bill, please.

khît-ngen-duài.

คิดเงินด้วย.

I think there's a mistake.

chán-khît-wà-phït

ฉันคิดว่าผิด.

Is service included in the bill ?

ruam-khă-bor-ri-kan-duài-roé-pläo?

รวมค่าบริการด้วยหรือเปล่า ?

Good evening, I'd like a table for two.

sä-wad-dee-chán-yăk-daì-tô-sám-räb-sorng-khon.

สวัสดี ฉันอยากได้โต๊ะสำหรับสองคน.

Could we have a table by the window.

- in the corner.

- on the terrace.

khor-tô - khàng nà-täng - dai-mái.

- mum-horng

- theè râ-biang.

ขอโต๊ะ ข้างหน้าต่าง ได้ไหม ?

- มุมห้อง

- ที่ระเบียง

Breakfast

breakfast
a-hán-châo
อาหารเช้า

What time is breakfast ?
we-la-a-hán-châo-këe-mong ?
เวลาอาหารเช้ากี่โมง ?

7 o'clock.
jed-na-ri-ka.
เจ็ดนาฬิกา.

Where is the breakfast room ?
hòrng-a-hán-châo-yoo-theè-nai ?
ห้องอาหารเช้าอยู่ที่ไหน ?

This way, please.
chern-thang-nêe.
เชิญทางนี้.

Breakfast is ready.
a-hán-châo-phrôrm-lâew.
อาหารเช้าพร้อมแล้ว.

What do you have for breakfast ?
mee-a-rai-bàng-sám-rab-a-hán-châo ?
มีอะไรบ้างสำหรับอาหารเช้า ?

Do you like coffee or tea ?
Which do you prefer, coffee or tea ?
khun-chòrb-ka-fae-roé-cha ?

คุณชอบกาแฟหรือชา ?

I like coffee.

chán-chòrb-ka-fae.

ฉันชอบกาแฟ.

I prefer tea.

chán-chòrb-cha.

ฉันชอบชา

Do you like it strong or weak ?

khun-chòrb-käe-roé-örn.

คุณชอบแก่หรืออ่อน ?

With cream ?

säi-khreem-maí ?

ใส่ครีมไหม ?

With sugar ?

sai-nâm-tan-maí ?

ใส่น้ำตาลไหม ?

I take my tea with sugar and cream.

chán-chòrb-cha-säi-nâm-tan-lâe-khreem.

ฉันชอบชาใส่น้ำตาลและครีม.

I want two soft-boiled eggs.

chán toȓng-kan-khäi-luàk-soŕng-forng.

ฉันต้องการไข่ลวก 2 ฟอง.

I want two hard-boiled eggs.

chán-toȓng-kan-khäi-tòm-soŕng-forng.

ฉันต้องการไข่ต้ม 2 ฟอง.

I want ham and eggs.

chán toȓng-kan-moó-haem-kab-khäi.

ฉันต้องการหมูแฮมกับไข่

I want toast.

- some butter.
- cheese.
- jam.

chán toȓng-kan - khäi-nóm-pang-pìng
- noei
- noei-khaéng
- yaem

ฉันต้องการ - ขนมปังปิ้ง
- เนย
- เนยแข็ง
- แยม

Something else ?

yäng-oën-ëek-maí ?

อย่างอื่นอีกไหม ?

No, thank you.

maì-khörb-khun.

ไม่ ขอบคุณ.

I've had enough.

chán-ïm-lâew.

ฉันอิ่มแล้ว.

Lunch

a-hán-klang-wan.

อาหารกลางวัน.

At what time do you have lunch ?

khun-rab-pra-than-a-hán-klang-wan-we-la-a-rai ?

คุณรับประทานอาหารกลางวันเวลาอะไร ?

about 12.00 o'clock.

rao-thiàng.

ราวเที่ยง.

I'm hungry now.

chán-héw-lâew.

ฉันหิวแล้ว.

Where shall we have lunch ?

rao-ja-pai-kin-theè-naí-dee ?

เราจะไปกินที่ไหนดี ?

Let's go to a restaurant near by.

pai-rân-a-hán-klaì-klaì-kan-theř

ไปร้านอาหารใกล้ ๆ กันเถอะ.

Would you care for a glass of beer ?

khun-ja-döem-bia-säk-kaèw-noëng-maí ?

คุณจะดื่มเบียร์สักแก้วหนึ่งไหม ?

Thank you very much.

khörb-khun-màk.

ขอบคุณมาก.

What will you have, sir ?

khun-to̲r̀ng-ka̲n-á̲-rai ?

คุณต้องการอะไร ?

Soup and stew chicken.

sub-lâe-sä-too-kai.

ซุปและสตูไก่

Anything else ?

a-rai-ëek ?

อะไรอีก ?

No, thank you. I've had enough.

mai-khö̲r̲b-khun-chán-ïm-lâew.

ไม่ ขอบคุณ ฉันอิ่มแล้ว.

Dinner

a-hán-yen.

อาหารเย็น.

When will we have dinner ?

rao-ja-rab-pra-than-a-hán-yen-moeà-rai ?

เราจะรับประทานอาหารเย็นเมื่อไหร่ ?

7.00 P.M.

nöeng-thùm.

หนึ่งทุ่ม.

Let's dine out.

pai-kin-kan-khàng-nork-thër.

ไปกินกันข้างนอกเถอะ.

What shall we have for dinner ?

rao-ja-kin-a-ria-kan-dee ?

เราจะกินอะไรกันดี ?

We have soup, meat, chicken, vegetable and fruit.

rao-mee-sûp-noêa-kai-phäk-lâe-phón-la-mâi.

เรามีซุป, เนื้อ, ไก่, ผัก และผลไม้.

I enjoy this very much.

chán-chòrb-neè-màk.

ฉันชอบนี่มาก.

We don't have it in our country.

nai-pra-thèt-khórng-rao-maì-mee.

ในประเทศของเราไม่มี.

Please eat everything you like.

kin-thùk-yăng-theè-khun-chŏrb.

กินทุกอย่างที่คุณชอบ.

I like this melon. It's very sweet.

chán-chòrb-taeng-mo-wán-dee.

ฉันชอบแตงโม หวานดี.

Some more of it ?

tòrng-kan-ëek-maí ?

ต้องการอีกไหม ?

Tea	cha	ชา
Coffee	ka-fae	กาแฟ

What time is tea served ?
döem-nârm-cha-kan-we-la-naí ?
ดื่มน้ำชากันเวลาไหน ?

Between 4.00 and 5.00 p.m.
ra-wäng-bäi-sëe-mong-thoéng-hà-mong.
ระหว่างบ่าย 4 โมง - 5 โมง.

Let's have tea now.
ma-döem-nâm-cha-kan-thër.
มาดื่มน้ำชากันเถอะ.

Do you take strong or week tea ?
khun-chorb-cha-käe-roé-orn ?
คุณชอบชาแก่หรืออ่อน ?

With sugar or without sugar ?
säi-nâm-tan-roé-maì-sai-nâm-tan ?
ใส่น้ำตาลหรือไม่ใส่น้ำตาล ?

With cream or without cream ?
säi-khreem-roé-maì-säi-khreem ?
ใส่ครีมหรือไม่ใส่ครีม ?

There are toast, butter and jam.
mee-kha-nóm-pang-pìng-noei-lâe-yaem.
มีขนมปังปิ้ง เนย และแยม

Would you like some sandwiches ?

khun-tòrng-kan-saen-wich -maí ?

คุณต้องการแซนวิชไหม ?

Some more toast ?

kha-nóm-pang-ëek-maí ?

ขนมปังอีกไหม ?

No, thank you.

maì-khörb-khum.

ไม่ขอบคุณ.

Waiter, give me the bill.

boí-keb-ngern-duaì.

บ๋อยเก็บเงินด้วย.

In the Café and Bar

café	rân-ka-fae	ร้านกาแฟ
Please give me Can I have	khor	ขอ
- coffee	ka-fae	กาแฟ
- a cup of tea	cha-thuaì-noëng	ชาถ้วยหนึ่ง
- black tea	cha-dam	ชาดำ
- sandwitch	saen-wich	แซนด์วิช
- spaghetti	sa-pa-ket-teè	สปาเกตตี้
- ice cream	ai-ša-khreem	ไอศครีม
- omlette	khäi-dao	ไข่ดาว
- orange squash	nâm-sòm-khân	น้ำส้มคั้น
- fruit juice	nâm-phón-la-mâi	น้ำผลไม้

with cream ?
säi-khreem-mai ?
ใส่ครีมไหม ?

Yes, please.
säi.
ใส่.

No, thank you.
maí-khörb-khun.
ไม่ขอบคุณ.

Hot or iced ?
rôrn-roé-yen ?

ร้อนหรือเย็น ?

Hot, please.

ròrn.

ร้อน.

Iced, please.

yen.

เย็น.

table	tô-a-hán	โต๊ะอาหาร
Give me...	khoŕ...	ขอ...
- soup	sup	ซุป
- salad	sä-lat	สลัด
- meat stew	sä-too-noêa	สตูว์เนื้อ
- pork chops	sèe-khrong-moó	ซี่โครงหมู
- roast meat	noêa-yàng	เนื้อย่าง
- fried fish	pla-thòrd	ปลาทอด
- dish of rice with chicken	khàw-kab-kaï	ข้าวกับไก่
- scrambled eggs.	khaï-jiao	ไข่เจียว
- eggs with ham.	kaï-kab-moó-haem	ไก่กับหมูแฮม
- roast chicken.	kaï-yàng	ไก่ย่าง
- fresh fruit.	phón-la-mâi-söd	ผลไม้สด
- fruit slad.	sä-lat-phón-la-mâi	สลัดผลไม้
- pineapple	säb-pä-rôt	สับปะรด

Give me a second helping.

khoŕ-term-eëk-nöi.

ขอเติมอีกหน่อย.

Please help yourself.

prŏt-chuaì-tua-eng.

โปรดช่วยตัวเอง.

How about some more ?

term-eëk-maí ?

เติมอีกไหม ?

No, thanks.

mai-khörb-khun.

ไม่ขอบคุณ.

Yes, please. very delicious.

ä-roï̈-mäk-khoŕ-term-eëk.

อร่อยมาก ขอเติมอีก.

I enjoy it very much.

chán-chòrb-màk.

ฉันชอบมาก.

Bill please.

këb-ngeŕn-duaì.

เก็บเงินด้วย.

Shall we go ?

pai-kan-roé-yang ?

ไปกันหรือยัง ?

Let's go.

pai-ther

ไปเถอะ.

Thai Food

food	a-hán	อาหาร
Thai food	a-hán-thai	อาหารไทย
curry	kaeng-phët	แกงเผ็ด
chicken curry	kaeng-käi	แกงไก่
Pork curry	kaeng-moó	แกงหมู
meat curry	kaeng-nôea	แกงเนื้อ
rice	khàw	ข้าว
boiled rice	khàw-tòm	ข้าวต้ม
boiled rice with chicken	khàw-tòm-kai	ข้าวต้มไก่
boiled rice with pork	khàw-tòm-moó	ข้าวต้มหมู
Fried	thor̀t, phät	ทอด, ผัด
Fried rice	khàw-phät	ข้าวผัด
fried pork	moó-thor̀t	หมูทอด
Fried chicken	kaï-thor̀t	ไก่ทอด
Fried meat	nôea-thor̀t	เนื้อทอด
Fried fish	pla-thor̀t	ปลาทอด
egg	khai	ไข่
Fried eggs	khaï-daw	ไข่ดาว
Omelette	khaï-jiao	ไข่เจียว
hard-boiled egg	khaï-tòm	ไข่ต้ม
soft-boiled egg	khaï-luàk	ไข่ลวก
sweet and salty pork	moó-wán	หมูหวาน

Curry

curry	kaeng-pët	แกงเผ็ด

Kaeng-phët is real Thai food. It is rather hot for foreigners. It is eaten with rice. Coconut-milk and nam-phrik are cooked with meat which may be chicken, prok or beaf. When curry or kaeng-phët is prepared for foreigners, it will not be very hot and you will like it.

Chicken curry	kaeng-phët-kai	แกงเผ็ดไก่
Pork curry	kaeng-phët-móo	แกงเผ็ดหมู
Beaf curry	kaeng-phët-noêa	แกงเผ็ดเนื้อ
Fish-ball curry	kaeng-phët-loòk-chîn-pla	แกงเผ็ดลูกชิ้นปลา

Eggs

Egg	khaï	ไข่

Eggs can be prepared in different styles.

Fried egg	khaï-daw	ไข่ดาว
omelette	khaï-jiao	ไข่เจียว
Hard-boiled egg	khaï-tòm	ไข่ต้ม
Soft-boiled egg	khaï-luàk	ไข่ลวก

Fried Food

Fry	thort, phät	ทอด, ผัด
Fried food	a-hán-thòrt	อาหารทอด
Fried chicken	kaï-thòrt	ไก่ทอด
Fried pork	moó-thòrt	หมูทอด
Fried fish	pla-thòrt	ปลาทอด
Fried beef	noea-thòrt	เนื้อทอด

Rice

Rice	khao	ข้าว

Rice is an important to Thai people as bread is to western people. Rice can be cooked in different styles.

When we speak of rice, it means rice cooked with water which is taken away and we eat only rice which is already cooked.

Boiled rice	khaw-tòm	ข้าวต้ม

Boiled rice is rice cooked with water and is eaten with water. Boiled rice can be taken with omelette, fried meat and fickled vegetable.

When any kind of meat is cooked with boiled rice, it is called after the name of the meat. We usually put eggs in boiled rice together with little pepper as seasoning.

Boiled rice - with chicken	khaw-tòm-kaï	ข้าวต้มไก่
-with pork	khaw-tòm-moó	ข้าวต้มหมู
- with shrimp	khaw-tòm-kùng	ข้าวต้มกุ้ง
- with fish	khaw-tòm-pla	ข้าวต้มปลา
- with duck	khaw-tòm-pët	ข้าวต้มเป็ด
- with oister	khaw-tòm-hoí-nang-rom	ข้าวต้มหอยนางรม
Fried rice	khaw-phät	ข้าวผัด

Fried rice is rice fried with any kind of meat :- chicken, shrimp, pork, crab - with vegetables and sauce as seasoning. It is very delicious and eatable for foreigners.

Mee-krorb หมี่กรอบ

This is very delicious Thai dish for foreigners. It is vermicelli fried with pork, shrimp, soyabean and egg. It is served with pickled garlic, orange peal and soya bean.

Hor-mok ห่อหมก

This is another delicious Thai dish, prepared with fish, (chicken or prawn) and curry, wrapped in banana leaf and steamed. It should be taken immediately after being cooked.

Fruits and Vegetables

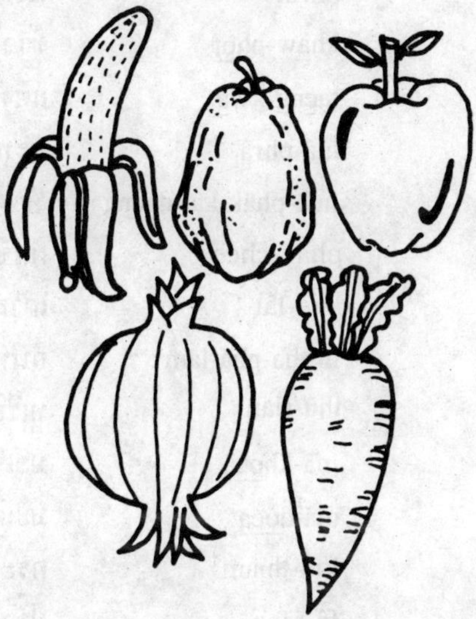

Fruits	phón-la-mâi	ผลไม้
Vegetables	phäk	ผัก
asparacus	nör-mâi	หน่อไม้
bale fruit	mâ-toom	มะตูม
bean sprout	thüa-ngoìrk	ถั่วงอก
banana	kluaì-hoŕm	กล้วยหอม
bullock's heart	nôi-nǒng	น้อยโหน่ง

cabbage	ka-läm-plee	กะหล่ำปลี
chili	phrìk	พริก
corn	khàw-phòt	ข้าวโพด
cucumber	taeng-kwa	แตงกวา
coconut	mâ-phrâ	มะพร้าว
carrot	huà-phäk-kat-daeng	หัวผักกาดแดง
coriander	phǟk-chee	ผักชี
chestnut	kao-lât	เกาลัด
date	in-tha-phá-lam	อินทผาลัม
durian	thû-rian	ทุเรียน
egg phant	mâ-khoeá	มะเขือ
fig	mâ-döea	มะเดื่อ
garlic	krä-thiam	กระเทียม
guava	fâ-räng	ฝรั่ง
gourd	nâm-taò	น้ำเต้า
ginger	khińg	ขิง
grape	a-ngün	องุ่น
jack fruit	khä-nún	ขนุน
lichee	lîn-jëe	ลิ้นจี่
longa	lam-yai	ลำไย
lansa	lang-sät	ลางสาด
lemon	mâ-na	มะนาว
lettuce	phäk-kät-hoŕm	ผักกาดหอม

marian plum	mâ-prang	มะปราง
musk melon	taeng-thai	แตงไทย
mango	mâ-muàng	มะม่วง
m ngosteen	longan mangosteen	มังคุด
mushroom	mang-khût	เห็ด
morning glory	hëd	ผักบุ้ง
orange	phäk-bùng	ส้ม
onion	sòm	หอม
papaya	hoŕm	มะละกอ
pumkin	mâ-lâ-kor	ฟักทอง
pepper	fâk-thorng	พริกไทย
persimmon	phrîk-thai	ลูกพลับ
pineapple	loòk-phlab	สับปะรด
pickled vegetables	säb-pä-rôt	ผักดอง
potato	phäk-dorng	มัน
pamelo	man	ส้มโอ
palm-fruit	sòm-oh	ลูกตาล
rambutan	loòk-tan	เงาะ
rose apple	ngôr	ชมพู่
spida	chom-phoò	มะไฟ
sandorica	mâ-fai	กระท้อน
sapota chico	kra-thôrn	ละมุด
sugar apple	la-mût	น้อยหน่า
	nôi-nä	

sugar cane	oì	อ้อย
turnip	húa-phäk-kät	หัวผักกาด
tomato	mâ-khoeá-thèt	มะเขือเทศ
tamarind	mâ-khám	มะขาม
water melon	taeng-mo	แตงโม

Trees and Flowers

Tree	tòn-mâi	ต้นไม้
Flower	dörk-mâi	ดอกไม้
leaf	bai-mâi	ใบไม้
root	ràk-mâi	รากไม้
to plant	plöok	ปลูก
garden	suán	สวน
bamboo	tôn-phaï	ต้นไผ่
jásmin	dörk-mâ-lî	ดอกมะลิ
dahlia	dörk-râk-rè	ดอกรักเร่
ilang ilang	dörk-kra-dang-nga	ดอกกระดังงา
lotus	dörk-bua	ดอกบัว
marigold	dörk-dao-roeng	ดอกดาวเรือง
orchid	dörk-kluaì-mâi	ดอกกล้วยไม้
French marigold	dörk-yeè-sün	ดอกยี่สุ่น
rose	dörk-ku-läb	ดอกกุหลาบ
sun flower	dörk-than-ta-wan	ดอกทานตะวัน

Animals

animal	sät	สัตว์
amphibian	sät-loêai-khlan	สัตว์เลื้อยคลาน
wild animal	sät-pä	สัตว์ป่า
alligator	jä-râ-khè	จระเข้
domestic animal	sät-liang	สัตว์เลี้ยง
crocodile	jä-râ-khè	จระเข้
zoo	suán-sät	สวนสัตว์

ant	môd	มด
antilope	kwang	กวาง
bat	khâng-khao	ค้างคาว
baboon	ling	ลิง
bee	phoèng	ผึ้ง
bear	meé	หมี
beatle	täo-thorng	เต่าทอง
worm	nońn	หนอน
buffalo	kwai	ควาย
butterfly	pheé-soeà	ผีเสื้อ
cat	maew	แมว
camel	öot	อูฐ
chimpanzee	ling	ลิง
cricket	jïng-rëet	จิ้งหรีด
cow	wua	วัว
crab	poo-tha-le	ปูทะเล
dog	su-nâk	สุนัข
deer	kwang	กวาง
elephant	châng	ช้าง
frog	kob	กบ
fox	su-nâk-pä	สุนัขป่า
goat	kae	แกะ
gorilla	ling	ลิง

hippopotamus	chậng-nậm	ช้างน้ำ
horse	mâ	ม้า
insect	mä-laeng	แมลง
kangaroo	jing-jò	จิงโจ้
lizard	jìng-jök	จิ้งจก
	kìng-kä	กิ้งก่า
lion	síng-to	สิงโต
lobster	kùng	กุ้ง
rat	noó	หนู
donkey	la	ลา
	mor̀t	มอด
monkey	ling	ลิง
boar	moó-pä	หมูป่า
oyster	hoí-nang-rom	หอยนางรม
ox	wuea	วัว
prawn	kùng-nang	กุ้งนาง
pig	moó	หมู
rabbit	kra-täi	กระต่าย
seal	nak	นาค
sea fish	pla-tha-le	ปลาทะเล
sheep	käe	แกะ
shell	hoí	หอย
squirrel	kra-roŕk	กระรอก

snake	ngoo	งู
spider	ma-<u>lae</u>ng-mum	แมลงมุม
tiger	<u>soeá</u>	เสือ
turtle	täo	เต่า
wolf	su-nâk-jìng-j<u>ör</u>k	สุนัขจิ้งจอก
zebra	m<u>â</u>-lai	ม้าลาย

The names of Interesting Places

names	choè	ชื่อ
interesting	nà-són-jai	น่าสนใจ
places	sä-thán-theè	สถานที่

Empassy

sä-thán-ëk-äk-kha-ràt-cha-thoòt สถานเอกอัครราชทูต

Legation	sä-thán-thoot	สถานทูต
Ministry	krä-suang	กระทรวง
Ministry of...	krä-suang...	กระทรวง...
- Foreign Affair	- täng-pra-thèt	- ต่างประเทศ
- Economic Affair	- sët-thâ-kan	- เศรษฐการ
- Education	- söek-sa-thî-kan	- ศึกษาธิการ
- Public Health	- sa-tha-ra-na-sük	- สาธารณสุข
- Communication	- khom-ma-na-khom	- คมนาคม
- Industry	- üd-sá-ha-kam	- อุตสาหกรรม

Public Relation Department.

krom-pra-cha-sám-phan.

กรมประชาสัมพันธ์

Department of Fine arts.

krom-sín-ra-pa-korn.

กรมศิลปากร

Custom Department

krom-sún-ra-ka-korn

กรมศุลกากร

Revenue Department
krom-sán-pha-korn
กรมสรรพากร
Police Department
krom-tam-rüad
กรมตำรวจ
Burean of the Royal Household
sam-nak-phrâ-rat-cha-wang
สำนักพระราชวัง
Hospital
rong-pha-ya-ban
โรงพยาบาล
Central Hospital
rong-pha-ya-ban-klang
โรงพยาบาลกลาง
Police Hospital
rong-pha-ya-ban-tam-rüad
โรงพยาบาลตำรวจ
Military Hospital
rong-pha-ya-ban-phra-mong-küt
โรงพยาบาลพระมงกุฎ
asylum
rong-pha-ya-ban-ròk-jiïd
โรงพยาบาลโรคจิต

Nerve Hospital
rong-pha-ya-ban-ròk-prä-sät
โรงพยาบาลโรคประสาท

Police Station	sa-thá-nee-tam-rüad	สถานีตำรวจ
University	ma-há-wit-ta-ya-lai	มหาวิทยาลัย
Çollege	wit-ta-ya-lai	วิทยาลัย
school	rong-rian	โรงเรียน
Cinema, movie	pab-pa-yon, rong-pab-pa-yon	ภาพยนตร์, โรงภาพยนตร์
Theatre	la-khorn, rong-la-khorn	ละคร โรงละคร
Restaurant	phât-ta-khan ı	ภัตตาคาร
Food shop	rân-a-hán	ร้านอาหาร
Coffee-shop	rân-ka-fae	ร้านกาแฟ
Dispensary, Drug store	rân-khaí-ya	ร้านขายยา
Monastery	wât	วัด
Temple	wât, bod	วัด, โบสถ์
Bank	tha-na-khan	ธนาคาร
money changer	theè-rab-laek-ngern	ที่รับแลกเงิน
Air port	thà-a-kät-sa-yan	ท่าอากาศยาน
Wharf	thà-roea	ท่าเรือ
zoo	suán-sät	สวนสัตว์

Park	suán-sátha-râ-nâ	สวนสาธารณะ
Hotel	rong-raen	โรงแรม
Home	bàn	บ้าน
Ocean	ma-há-sa-müt	มหาสมุทร
sea	ta-le	ทะเล
river	maè-nâm	แม่น้ำ
Canal	khlorng	คลอง
gulf	äo	อ่าว
Island	kör	เกาะ
stream	lam-than	ลำธาร
ditch	khoo	คู
Pond	sa-nâm	สระน้ำ
well	bör	บ่อ
lake	ta-le-säb	ทะเลสาบ
water fall	nâm-tök	น้ำตก
mountain	phoo-kháo	ภูเขา
Air Travel office	sám-nâk-ngan -dern-a-kät	สำนักงาน เดินอากาศ

Sight seeing

There are many interesting places in Thailand. Most tourists who visit our country go with the tour which take care of all their needs. However, for those who don't, may read the followings in order to know about some interesting places worth visiting.

Wat Phra Sriratana Sasadaram, generally know as Wat Phra Kaeo.

1. The Grand Palace and Wat Phra Kaew

Wat Phra kae is also called the Temple of Emerald Buddha. The grand Palace and Wat Phra Kaew are adjoining in a big compound on Na Phra Lan Road near Phramane Grand, surrounded by high white walls.

The palace, built in 1788, consists of several buildings with highly decorated architecture. The King and Queen do not live in the Palace which is used for other things. The great Court is used for the Ministry of Finance· On the east side is Sala Sahathai Samakhom which is used for reception purposes. The Hall of Dusit is used as an audience hall; the Chakree Hall was by a British architecture in European Style with a Thai style roof. The top floor contains golden earns with ashes of the decreased Kings of the Chakree Dynastry. The second floor contains reception room which leads to the private room for their Majesties to receive individual guests.

Wat Phra Kaew, the Royal chapel, honeses the Emerald Buddha, the most sacred Buddha image in Thailand which is made of jespar, has three sets of costumes, one for the hot season; one for the raining season and one for the cool season, each costume is changed at the begining cool season by the King himself. Taking photographs inside the building housing the Emerald Buddha is not allowed.

The Grand Palace is open everyday and closed on official days, but on Saturdays and Sundays only the exterior area is open to public. Proper dress is required on all occation.

2. The National Museum

This is one of the largest museums in Southeast Asia. It is near the Grand Palace. The complex, also built in 1782, consists of several old and beautiful buildings of colourful Thai architecture.

The Museum is open everyday except Mondays and Fridays.

3. Temple of Reclining Buddha (Wat-Po)

This is located on the south of the Grand Palace. It is one of the oldest and largest temples in Bangkok, and is also called Thailand's First University, the first centre of public education, literature, archaeology and astrology.

The association of the traditional medical school of Thailand is in Wat Po. Traditional massage is also practiced, and there are statues of hermits demonstrating various positions of massage.

Wat Po was built by King Rama 1 nearly 200 years ago and houses the big gold plated Reclining Buddha, 160 feet-long and 40 feet high.

The Replica of Phra Buddha Chinaraj (The Marble Temple Wat Benjama bopit)

4. The Marble Temple (Wat Benjamabophit)

This is on Sri Ayudhaya Road near the National Assembly building. It is constructed of Italian marble during the reign of King Rama V in Thai style designed and supervised by Prince Naris, the great artist and architect of the period.

The main building is open to visitors every day with no admission charge.

5. The temple of The Dawn (Wat Arun)

This is on the bank of the Thonburi side of the Chao Phaya River. construction of the Temple began in reign of King Rama II and completed by King Rama III. It consists of five Prangs with embroided pottery fragments arranged in floral patterns; the tallest Prang is about 22`feet high. It looks most beautiful at dawn and at sunset.

Golden Buddha of Wat Trimit

6. The temple of the Golden Buddha (Wat Traimit)

Wat Traimit is on Traimit Road, not far from Bangkok Railway Station. It is known for its Golden Buddha, three meters high and weighs five and a half ton. It is believed that the golden Buddha was constructed during Sukhothai period. The temple is open everyday with no admision fee.

7. The Royal Throne Hall

The Royal Throne Hall is a magnificent structure made of marble by the other of King Chulalongkorn in European style. Within the great hall is a nineteired ceremonial umbrella, the symbol of the King's authority. It was used for the meeting of the national assembly until recently.

8. The National Theatre

This is on Na Phra Lan Road next to the National Museum. There will be classical dramas and other types of international arts here from time to time. Special exhibition shows of Thai classical dance and music are held on the evening of the last Friday of each month.

9. The Rose Garden

This is 32 kms. south of Bangkok on the banks of the Thajeen river. It is popular for its beautiful garden and ideal for a picnic in a Country Resort. In the garden there are a Thai cultural village, demonstration of elephant at work, spinning and weaving silk thread into materials of beautiful colours and designs, and cultural show of sword fighting, etc.

The garden is open daily.

10. The Ancient City

The city covers the area of some 200 acres in considered the world's largest out door museum. It consists of replicas of many of the most-famous buildings, monuments, and temples to be found in all parts of Thailand. It is located at km 33 on the Sukhumvit Highways in Samut Prakarn Province. The city is open every day and vehicles are available in the city to convey visitors through its large area.

11. The Floating Markets

This is very important commercial Centre for people along the banks of the canals. The Floating Markets are usually crowded with small boats packed with all kinds of tropical fruits, vegetables and other products from the orchards or nearly communities.

The first Floating Market is the Wat Sai Market in Bangkok and the other is the Damneon Saduak Market in Rajaburee, some 80 kms. south-west of Bangkok.

1. Phra Pathom Chedi

This Chedi or Pagoda is in Nakorn Pathom, 50 kms. from Bangkok. It is the largest, hightest and oldest in Thailand.

Phra Pathom chedi can be reached by bus, train and car everyday.

2. Ayudthaya and Bang Pa-in Summer Palace

Ayudthaya, the capital of Thailand for 417 years, is 70-88 kms. north of Bangkok. It was founded by King U-Thorng in the year 1350 and fell by the Burmese in 1767 at present, many ruins still exist while some are restored. Ayudthaya can be reached by train, bus, car and boat.

The beautiful Bang Pa-in Summer Palace, some 47 kms. from Ayudthaya was built 300 years ago and was reconstructed in the reign of King Rama V. The Palace consists of several buildings in various styles—Thai, Chinese, Italian and Victoria The landscape of the palace grounds is beautifully done. The palace can be reached by bus or car. The grounds are open everyday except Monday and Friday.

3. Surin

This is in the Northeast part of Thailand. There have been elephant show every year. A hundred of elephants are on the show which consists of the Rochet-Dance. The demonstration of wild animals, running a race, a Tug. of War between an elephant and one hundred soldiers and Elephant battle.

4. Phuket

Phuket is an island off the west coast of Thailand in the Andaman Sea. It is a beautiful, peaceful and restful place with fine beaches and crystal blue water. There is also a place where giant sea-turtles were bred and come up to lay there eggs. From Phuket one can cruise to the neighbouring island.

Phra Buddha Sihing, Chiang Mai

Finished parasols at Bo Sang

5. Chieng Mai

In Chieng Mai, the ancient capital city of Northern Thailand with its own culture and charm, there are many interesting things and places. It is enjoyable climbing up 390 steps to Wat Phra Thart Doi Suthep on the top of the hill. There are also beautiful water falls, interesting elephant demonstration, the umbrella making, the factories of celadon pottery and weaving.

Tourist Policeman patrolling beach in Pattaya

7. Pattaya

This is one of the loveliest seaside resorts where water sports are abundant—fishing, sailing, swimming and water—skiing. Other out door sports—golf, tennis, horse—riding and indoor sports—bowling, chess or exercising in a gym, are also available.

8. Hua-Hin on sea

Hua-Hin is a small fishing town and seaside resort on the Gulf of Thailand about 200 kms. to the south of Bangkok. It can be reached by car, bus and train to walk along the beach, to collect shells and go swimming. There are also a good golf court and fishing boats for fishing or riding.

9. Karnjanaburee

The town is located on the River Kwai , where travellers will be impressed by its historical significance. During World War II, The Japanese brought many prisoners of war to this area to build a railroad to Burma. The railway is called the Death Railway because thousands of allied prisoners of war were dead during its construction and more than 8,000 prisoners of war were burried.

Beside the Death Railway another war evidence is the War Museum at Wat Chaichumphon where there are collections of arms ammunitions and photographs taken during the second World War, and the collection of varian types of engines being used during the time.

Is there a coach tour of the town ?
Mee-rôd-pha-chom-sa-thán-theè-nai-muang-maí ?
มีรถพาชมสถานที่ในเมืองไหม ?
Can we take a boat trip on the river ?
rao-pai-tiaò-thang-roea-daì-maí ?
เราไปเที่ยวทางเรือได้ไหม ?
Is there a guide ?
me-khon-nam-tiaò-maí ?
มีคนนำเที่ยวไหม ?
Is there any thing of interest ?
mee-a-rai-nà-són-jai-bàng ?
มีอะไรน่าสนใจบ้าง ?
What do you recommend us to visit ?
khun-ja-nâe-nam-hāi-pai-theè-naí-bàng ?
คุณจะแนะนำให้ไปที่ไหนบ้าง ?
Is the museum open everyday ?
phi-phît-tha-phan-pērd-thook-wan-maí ?
พิพิธภัณฑ์เปิดทุกวันไหม ?

How much is the admission ?
khà̱-doo-thaò-rai ?
ค่าดูเท่าไร ?

Is admission free ?
maỉ-tòng-sỉa-khà̱-doo-roé ?
ไม่ต้องเสียค่าดูหรือ ?

I would like to go to the temple.
chán-yä̱k-pai-wât.
ฉันอยากไปวัด.

Do you have any good guide book ?
mee-náng-so̱é-nam-thiàw-dee-dee-maí ?
มีหนังสือนำเที่ยวดี ๆ ไหม ?

Is there any tourist office ?
mee-sám-nâk-nga̱n-thoȑng-thiàw-mai ?
มีสำนักงานท่องเที่ยวไหม ?

Where is the tourist information centre ?
soón-ka̱n-thoȑng-thiàw-yöo-theè-naí ?
ศูนย์การท่องเที่ยวอยู่ที่ไหน ?

What are the most interesting ?
mee-a-rai-nà-són-jai-theè-süd ?
มีอะไรน่าสนใจที่สุด ?

Where should we go around and about ?
rao-ja-pai-doo-a-rai-kan-dee ?
เราจะไปดูอะไรกันดี ?

Where can we take the bus ?
rao-ja-pai-khoèn-rôd-daì-theè-naí ?
เราจะไปขึ้นรถได้ที่ไหน ?

Will the bus pick us up to the hotel ?
rôd-ja-ma-râb-rao-theè-rong-raem-maí ?
รถจะมารับเราที่โรงแรมไหม ?

Have we to go by train ?
rao-ja-torng-pai-rôd-fai-róe ?
เราจะต้องไปรถไฟหรือ ?

How much does the tour cost ?
siá-khá-rôd-thaò-räi ?
เสียค่ารถเท่าไร ?

At what time does the tour start ?
rôd-ork-we-la-naí ?
รถออกเวลาไหน ?

Can we rent a car for a day ?
rao-chào-rôd-pai-thâng-wan-dai-mái ?
เราเช่ารถไปทั้งวันได้ไหม ?

How can we go to the museum ?
rao-ja-pai-phi-phît-tha-phan-dai-yäng-rai ?
เราจะไปพิพิธภัณฑ์ได้อย่างไร ?

What's that building ?
nàn-a-khan-a-rai ?
นั่นอาคารอะไร ?

Where is the Parliament ?
rat-thâ-sä-pha-yöo-theè-naí ?
รัฐสภาอยู่ที่ไหน ?

It's very

- interesting	nà-són-jai-màk	น่าสนใจมาก
- amazing	nà-phît-sä-wóng	น่าพิศวง
- magnificent	yäi-to-pen-sä-ngä	ใหญ่โตเป็นสง่า
- strange	pläek-prä-läd	แปลกประหลาด
- terrible	nà-klua	น่ากลัว
- agly	nà-kliad	น่าเกลียด
- beautiful	suaí-ngam	สวยงาม

Is the temple of Emeral Buddha far away ?
wât-phra-kaèw-yöo-klai-maí ?
วัดพระแก้วอยู่ไกลไหม ?

Is it open every day ?
pert-thuk-wan-roé ?
เปิดทุกวันหรือ ?

Is it open only on Sunday ?
pert-chä-phôr-wan-a-thit-róe ?
เปิดเฉพาะวันอาทิตย์หรือ ?

Shall we get in the temple ?
khaò-pai-khàng-nai-wât-kan-maí ?
เข้าไปข้างในวัดกันไหม ?

I would like to walk around.
chán-ya̱k-dern-doo-ro̱rb-ro̱rb
ฉันอยากเดินดูรอบ ๆ

What about those paining on the wall ?
phàb-khián-bon-pha-náng-nân-ro̱ea̱ṉg-a-rai ?
ภาพเขียนบนผนังนั้นเรื่องอะไร ?

Are there prists in the temple ?
me-phra-yöo-nai-wat-maií ?
มีพระอยู่ในวัดไหม ?

Am I allowed to get into the Temple ?
chán-khaò-pai-nai-wât-dai-maí ?
ฉันเข้าไปในวัดได้ไหม ?

Are foreignes allowed to get into the Temple ?
chaw-täng-pra-thèt-khaò-pai-nai-wât-dai-maí ?
ชาวต่างประเทศเข้าไปในวัดได้ไหม ?

Are Buddhist temples opened to all ?
wât-phût-tha-sa̱t-sä-ná̱-pë̱ṟt-hai-tûk-khon-khaò-ró̱e̱ ?
วัดพุทธศาสนาเปิดให้ทุกคนเข้าหรือ ?

Is over there building the Grand Palace ?
töek-nân-kho̱e̱-phra-ba-rom-ma-há̱-rà̱d-châ-wang-chaì-maí ?
ตึกนั้นคือพระบรมมหาราชวังใช่ไหม ?

Let's go to the Grand Palace now, shall we ?
rao-pai-phra-ba-rom-ma-há̱-ra̱d-chà-wang-kan-maí ?
เราไปพระบรมมหาราชวังกันไหม ?

Do the King and Queen live in the Grand Palace ?

Phra-bat-sóm-det-phrâ-chao-yöo-huá-lâe-sóm-det-phra-ba-rom-
ma-ra-chî-nee-pra-tâb-nai-phra-ba-rom-ma-há-rat-châ-wang-roé ?

พระบาทสมเด็จพระเจ้าอยู่หัวและสมเด็จฯ พระบรมราชินี
ประทับในพระบรมมหาราชวังหรือ ?

We have such a wonderful trip today, didn't we ?

rao-tiaò-kan-sä-nuk-mak-wan-nêe.

เราเที่ยวกันสนุกมากวันนี้.

I enjoy the trip and appreciate your accompany very much.

chán-choŕb-kan-tiaò-wan-nêe-màk-lâe-khörb-khun-theè-ma-kab
-chán-duaì.

ฉันชอบการเที่ยววันนี้มากและขอบคุณที่มากับฉันด้วย.

May I take photograph ?

chán-ja-thäi-roob-daì-maí ?

ฉันจะถ่ายรูปได้ไหม ?

Where is the theatre/cinema ?

rong-la-khorn/rong-náng-yöo-theè-nái ?

โรงละคร/โรงหนังอยู่ที่ไหน ?

When does the theatre start ?

la-korn-lèn-moèa-rai ?

ละครเล่นเมื่อไร ?

What film is playing tonight ?

khoen-nêe-náng-roèang-a-rai ?

คืนนี้หนังเรื่องอะไร ?

I would like to visit a nightclub.
chán-ya̱k-pai-nâit-khlâb.
ฉันอยากไปไนท์คลับ.

Where do we go shopping ?
rao-ja-pai-sô̱e-kho̱rng-kan-theè-nái ?
เราจะไปซื้อของกันที่ไหน ?

Do you know any good department store ?
khun-rôo-jak-ha̱ng-sap-phâ-sín-khâ̱-dee-dee-maí ?
คุณรู้จักห้างสรรพสินค้าดี ๆ ไหม ?

We would like to go sightseeing.
rao-ya̱k-pai-chom-sä-thá̱n-theè-nai-mo̱e̱ang.
เราอยากไปชมสถานที่ในเมือง

How can we do ?
rao-ja-tham-ya̱ng-rai ?
เราจะทำอย่างไร ?

You can take a taxi.
pai-rôd-räb-jà̱ng.
ไปรถรับจ้าง.

You drive around slowly.
khäb-pai-ro̱rb-ro̱rb-châ-châ.
ขับไปรอบ ๆ ช้า ๆ .

Get me a taxi.
riak-rôd-räb-jà̱ng-hai-chán-duai.
เรียกรถรับจ้างให้ฉันด้วย.

What's that ?

nàn-a-rai ?

นั่นอะไร ?

What's that on your right/left ?

nân-a-rai-thang-khwá/thang-sâi ?

นั่นอะไรทางขวา/ทางซ้าย ?

What's that in front ?

khàng-nä-nân-a-rai ?

ข้างหน้านั่นอะไร ?

Where's the road leading to ?

tha-nón-nêe-pai-naí ?

ถนนนี้ไปไหน ?

Drive straight forward.

khäb-trong-pai.

ขับตรงไป.

Turn to the left. Stop here a minute.

liâw-sâi. yüt-trong-nêe-pra-diaẃ.

เลี้ยวซ้าย. หยุดตรงนี้ประเดี๋ยว.

Travelling By Train

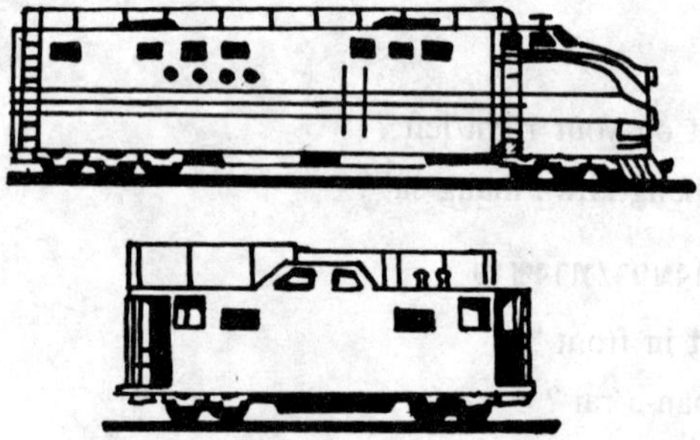

If you want to travel by train you have to go to the railway station, buy your ticket and go to the plat-form where your train is parking. If you have heavy trucks or suitcases, the proter will help you. Sitting on the train, the guard will check your ticket.

Taxi, take me to the railway station.
pha̱-chán-pai-sa-thá̱-nee-rôd-fai.
พาฉันไปสถานีรถไฟ.
Where is the ticket office ?
hòng-khaí-tuá̱-yöo-theè-naí ?
ห้องขายตั๋วอยู่ที่ไหน ?
How much is the fare ?
khä̱-rôd-thaò-rai ?
ค่ารถเท่าไร ?

Give me two first class tickets.
sôe-tuá-chân-nöeng-sórng-bai.
ซื้อตั๋วชั้นหนึ่ง 2 ใบ.

Put them on the rack.
ao-wang-wai-bon-hiǹg.
เอาวางไว้บนหิ้ง.

The train is very crowded.
rôd-fai-naèn-màk.
รถไฟแน่นมาก.

At what time does the train leave ?
rôd-fai-örk-moeà-rai ?
รถไฟออกเมื่อไร ?

Is it a through train ?
neè-rôd-düan-roé ?
นี่รถด่วนหรือ ?

Is this the right plat-form ?
chan-cha-la-nêe-chaì-maí ?
ชานชาลานี้ใช่ไหม ?

What is the next station ?
sa-thá-nee-tör-pai-khoe-sa-thánee-a-rai ?
สถานีต่อไปคือสถานีอะไร ?

Don't lean out of the window.
yä-cha-ngòk-örk-pai-nòrk-nà-täng.
อย่าชะโงกออกไปนอกหน้าต่าง.

Ticket. please.
khoŕ-doo-tuá.
ขอดูตั๋ว.
How long will the train stop here ?
rôd-fai-ja-yüt-theè-neè-nan-thaò-rai ?
รถไฟจะหยุดที่นี่นานเท่าไร ?
Does the train stop at every station ?
rôd-yüd-thôok-sa-thá-nee-roé ?
รถหยุดทุกสถานีหรือ ?
What is the last station ?
sa-thá-nee-sut-thâi-koe-sa-thá-nee-a-rai ?
สถานีสุดท้ายคือสถานีอะไร ?
When will we reach… ?
moè-rai-ja-thoéng… ?
เมื่อไรจะถึง... ?
Would you make up our bed ?
ja-tham-theè-norn-roe ?
จะทำที่นอนหรือ ?
Can you help me with my bags ?
chuaì-ao-kra-paó-long-duaì ?
ช่วยเอากระเป๋าลงด้วย ?

Travelling by Bus

Where can I get a bus to… 1

chân-ja-khoèn-rôd-pra-jam-thang-pai…..daì-theè-naí ?

ฉันจะขึ้นรถประจำทางไป....ได้ที่ไหน ?

What bus can I take ?

chán-ja-toŕng-khoèn-rôd-a-rai ?

ฉันจะต้องขึ้นรถอะไร ?

Where's the bus stop terminal ?

plai-tang-rôd-yöu-theè-nái ?

ปลายทางรถอยู่ที่ไหน ?

How often do the buses to…run ?

rôd-pai…örk-böi-mái ?

รถไป...ออกบ่อยไหม ?

How long does the journey take ?

rôd-laèn-nan-thaò-rai ?

รถแล่นนานเท่าไร ?

Do I have to change buses ?

tor̀ng-pliän-rôd-maí ?

ต้องเปลี่ยนรถไหม ?

I want to get off at…

chàn-ja-long-theè…

ฉันจะลงที่....

Will you tell me when to get off.

chuai-bork-duai-moea-thoèng-theè-long.

ช่วยบอกด้วยเมื่อถึงที่ลง.

Please let me off at the next stop.

khoŕ-long-paì-nà.

ขอลงป้ายหน้า.

May I have my Baggage, please.

khoŕ-kra-pao-duaì.

ขอกระเป๋าด้วย.

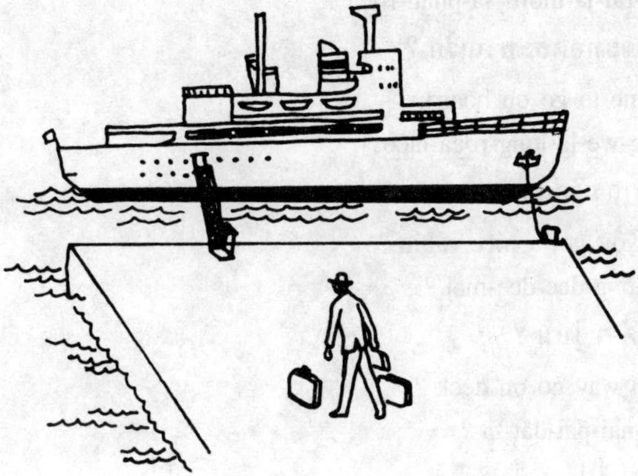

Where can I buy a ticket ?
chán-ja-pai-sôe-túa-dai-theè-nai ?
ฉันจะไปซื้อตั๋วได้ที่ไหน ?
Which class are you travelling ?
khun-jä-pai-chân-naí ?
คุณจะไปชั้นไหน ?
When will the boat leave ?
roea-jä-örk-möea-rai ?
เรือจะออกเมื่อไร ?

When is the gangway round ?

möea-rai-ja-thord-sa-phan-roea ?

เมื่อไรจะทอดสะพานเรือ ?

It's time to go on board.

thoéng-we-la-long-roea-laêo.

ถึงเวลาลงเรือแล้ว.

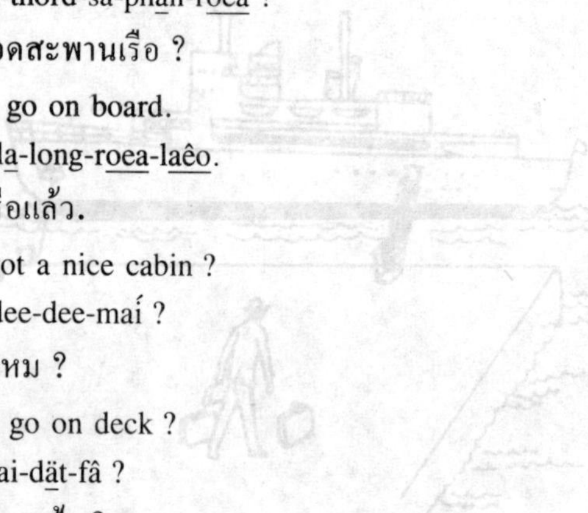

Have you got a nice cabin ?

mee-hòng-dee-dee-maí ?

มีห้องดี ๆ ไหม ?

Which way go on deck ?

thang-naí-pai-dät-fâ ?

ทางไหนไปดาดฟ้า ?

Let's go on deck.

khoen-pai-dät-fâ-kan-thër.

ขึ้นไปดาดฟ้ากันเถอะ.

I want to hire a deck chair.

chán-yäk-chaò-kaò-eè-bon-dät-fâ.

ฉันอยากเช่าเก้าอี้บนดาดฟ้า.

The sea is smooth/rough.

ta-le-riàb/mee-khloèn-jät.

ทะเลเรียบ/มีคลื่นจัด.

I'm sea sick.

chán-mao-khloèn.

ฉันเมาคลื่น.

I'll vomit.

chán-jä-ajian.

ฉันจะอาเจียน

Is there a life-belt ?

mee-khem-khät-choo-cheèp-maí ?

มีเข็มขัดชูชีพไหม ?

Can I have meals in my cabin ?

chán-rab-pra-than-a-hán-nai-hòng-daì-maí ?

ฉันรับประทานอาหารในห้องได้ไหม ?

How many passengers do we have ?

mee-phoò-doiy-sán-kee-khon ?

มีผู้โดยสารกี่คน ?

I'll disembark now.

chán-jä-khoèn-jäk-roea-diáw-nêe-laêw.

ฉันจะขึ้นจากเรือเดี๋ยวนี้แล้ว.

I enjoy travelling by boat.

chán-chorb-dern-thang-thang-reoa.

ฉันชอบเดินทางทางเรือ.

It's an enjoyable trip.

pen-kan-thorng-thiaw-theè-sa-nük.

เป็นการท่องเที่ยวที่สนุก.

Going to the Cinema

I would like to go to the cinema.
chán-yăk-pai-doo-phab-pha-yon.
ฉันอยากไปดูภาพยนตร์.

I don't know where the cinema is.
chán-mai-rôo-wà-rong-pab-pha-yon-yöo-theè-nai ?
ฉันไม่รู้ว่าโรงภาพยนตร์อยู่ที่ไหน ?

What's on today ?
wan-nêe-chaí-roèang-a-rai ?
วันนี้ฉายเรื่องอะไร ?

Will you go with me ?
pai-käb-chán-maí ?
ไปกับฉันไหม ?

Let's go now.
pai-kan-thër.
ไปกันเถอะ.

What's showing now ?
kam-lang-chaí-roèang-a-rai ?
กำลังฉายเรื่องอะไร ?

Where is the ticket office ?
hòng-khaí-tuá-yöo-theè-naí ?
ห้องขายตั๋วอยู่ที่ไหน ?

I want two seats.
chán-toŕng-kan-soŕng-theè-nàng.
ฉันต้องการ 2 ที่นั่ง.

When does the show begin ?

náng-jä-chaí-moeà-rai ?

หนังจะฉายเมื่อไร ?

When does it end ?

ler̀k-moeà-rai ?

เลิกเมื่อไร ?

That's the way in.

thang-khào-yöo-nàn.

ทางเข้าอยู่นั่น.

It's exciting.

nà-töen-tèn.

น่าตื่นเต้น.

The show has ended.

náng ler̀k-lâew.

หนังเลิกแล้ว.

That's the National Anthem.

phleng-san-ser̀n-phra-ba-ra-me-lâew.

เพลงสรรเสริญพระบารมีแล้ว.

Let's stand up.

yoen-khoèn.

ยืนขึ้น.

That's the way out.

thang-ork-yöo-nàn.

ทางออกอยู่นั่น.

Do you like newsreel ?

khun-chorb-náng-khäw-maí ?

คุณชอบหนังข่าวไหม ?

I like sports news.

chán-chorb-khäw-kee-ra.

ฉันชอบข่าวกีฬา.

Children like comedy and cartoon.

dëk-chorb-náng-ta-lök-lâe-ka-toon.

เด็กชอบหนังตลกและการ์ตูน.

What's playing at the Nation theatre ?

theè-röng-la-korn-häeng-chàt-kam-lang-sä-daeng-a-rai ?

ที่โรงละครแห่งชาติกำลังแสดงอะไร ?

Can you recommend - a good film ?
- a thriller ?
- something light ?

khun-nae-nam - roeang-dee-dee- dai-mai
- roeang-toen-ten- dai-mai
- roeang-bao-bao- dai-mai

คุณแนะนำ - เรื่องดี ๆ ได้ไหม ?
- เรื่องตื่นเต้น ได้ไหม ?
- เรื่องเบา ๆ ได้ไหม ?

At the theatre is that play now showing ?

la-korn-roeang-nân-kam-lang-lèn-theè-naí ?

ละครเรื่องนั้นกำลังเล่นที่ไหน ?

Who's playing ?

khrai-sä-daeng ?

ใครแสดง ?

Who's the director ?

khrai-pen-phoò-am-nuay-kan-sä-daeng ?

ใครเป็นผู้อำนวยการแสดง ?

What time does the show end ?

kan-sä-daeng-lèrk-moeà-rai ?

การแสดงเลิกเมื่อไร ?

Are there any tickets for tonight ?

yang-mee-bat-sám-räb-koen-nee-maí ?

ยังมีบัตรสำหรับคืนนี้ไหม ?

Can I book a ticket for tomorrow night ?

chán-jorng-tuá-koen-phrùng-nêe-dai-maí ?

ฉันจองตั๋วคืนพรุ่งนี้ได้ไหม ?

May I reserve two tickets for the show on Sunday night.

khór-jorng-tuá-khoen-wan-a-thit-soŕng-bai.

ขอจองตั๋วคืนวันอาทิตย์ 2 ใบ.

I want a seat not too far forward.

chán chor̀b-theè-nang-mai-nà-kern-pai.

ฉันชอบที่นั่งไม่หน้าเกินไป.

I like a seat somewhere in the middle.

chán-chor̀b-theè-nàng-klang-klang

ฉันชอบที่นั่งกลาง ๆ

May I have the programme, please ?

kh<u>or</u>-doo-pro-kram.

ขอดูโปรแกรม.

Did you enjoy yourself ?

khun-sä-nük-mai ?

คุณสนุกไหม ?

Can you recommend a good nightclub ?

khun-chuai-nâe-nam-nâit-khlub-dee-dee-dai-mai ?

คุณช่วยแนะนำไนท์คลับดี ๆ ได้ไหม ?

Is evening dress necessary ?

torng-taeng-chud-ra-tree-mai ?

ต้องแต่งชุดราตรีไหม ?

Is there a floor show ?

mee-kan-sä-daeng-bon-we-thee-mái ?

มีการแสดงบนเวทีไหม ?

At what time does the floor show start ?

kan-sä-daeng-bon-we-thee-rerm-këe-mong ?

การแสดงบนเวทีเริ่มกี่โมง ?

Do you like dancing ?

Would you like to dance ?

khun-chorb-tèn-ram-mai ?

คุณชอบเต้นรำไหม ?

Where can we go dancing ?

rao-ja-pai-tèn-ram-kan-theè-nai ?

เราจะไปเต้นรำกันที่ไหน ?

Is there a dance hall any where here ?

mee-sä-thán-theè-tèn-ram-thaéw-nêe-theè-nái-bàng ?

มีสถานที่เต้นรำแถวนี้ที่ไหนบ้าง ?

Shall we go to dance ?

Shall we dance ?

tèn-ram-kan-maí ?

เต้นรำกันไหม ?

May I have this dance ?

Would you dance with me ?

khoŕ-phóm-tèn-ram-kab-khun-thër ?

ขอผมเต้นรำกับคุณเถอะ.

May I have the honour to dance with you.

khoŕ-haì-phóm-mee-kiät-dài-tèn-ram-kab-khun.

ขอให้ผมมีเกียรติได้เต้นรำกับคุณ.

You dance very well/beautifully.

khun-tèn-ram-dai-dee-màk/suaí-màk.

คุณเต้นรำได้ดีมาก/สวยมาก.

I like to dance with you.

chan-chor̀b-tèn-ram-kab-khun.

ฉันชอบเต้นรำกับคุณ.

Let's sit out this dance.

yá-tèn-loei-phleng-nêe.

อย่าเต้นเลยเพลงนี้.

The floor is very crowded.

we-thee-naèn-màk.

เวทีแน่นมาก.

Are you tired ?

khun-noëai-maí ?

คุณเหนื่อยไหม ?

Radio and Television

radio	wit-tha-yû	วิทยุ
television	tho̲-ra-thât	โทรทัศน์

Would you like to listen to the radio ?

khun-cho̲rb-fang-wit-tha-yû-maí ?

คุณชอบฟังวิทยุไหม ?

I like to watch the television.

chan-cho̲rb-doo-tho̲-ra-thât.

ฉันชอบดูโทรทัศน์.

What is on the television tonight ?
tho-ra-thât-khoen-nêe-mee-a-rai ?
โทรทัศน์คืนนี้มีอะไร ?

Please switch on the radio.
chuaì-pert-wit-tha-yû-nöi.
ช่วยเปิดวิทยุหน่อย.

Have the television on, please ?
pert-tho-ra-thât-duài.
เปิดโทรทัศน์ด้วย.

Please turn it down.
rëe-haì-khoì-noï.
หรี่ให้ค่อยหน่อย.

A little louder, please.
haì-dang-ëek-nîd.
ให้ดังอีกนิด.

Make the picture clearer.
prab-phàb-haì-chat-khòen.
ปรับภาพให้ชัดขึ้น.

What would you like, news or music ?
khun-chorb-a-rai-khäw-roé-don-tree ?
คุณชอบอะไร ข่าวหรือดนตรี ?

I'd like to listen to the news.
chan-yäk-fang-khäw.
ฉันอยากฟังข่าว.

I prefer music to news.

chán chorb-don-tree-màk-kwa-khäw.

ฉันชอบดนตรีมากกว่าข่าว.

I prefer watching a play.

chán-chorb-doo-la-khorn.

ฉันชอบดูละคร.

Shall we turn to another channel ?

mún-pai-chorng-oën-maí ?

หมุนไปช่องอื่นไหม ?

Please turn to channel 9.

mún-pai-chorng-kaò.

หมุนไปช่องเก้า.

I'd like to listen to BBC.

chán-yäg-fang-bee-bee-see.

ฉันอยากฟังบีบีซี.

I'd like to go to bed now.

chán-yäk-norn-lâew.

ฉันอยากนอนแล้ว.

I'm fed up with it.

chán-boëa-lâew.

ฉันเบื่อแล้ว.

Turn it off then.

thà-yäng-nân-korָ-pit-siá.

ถ้าอย่างนั้นก็ปิดเสีย.

The addition to thai sports such as Boxing and Ta-kror, any western sports are also popular in Thailand. You can enjoy much games as football, rugby, basket-ball, base-ball and golf. We also have many swiming pools.

Do you care for sports and games ?

khun-chorb-kee-ra-maí ?

คุณชอบกีฬาไหม ?

I like watching them.

chán-chorb-doo.

ฉันชอบดู.

I like taking exercise in the

- moring.
- evening.

chán-chorb-ork-kam-lang-kai-torn-châo/yen.

ฉันชอบออกกำลังกายตอนเช้า/เย็น.

Which kind of sports do you like ?

khun-chorb-kee-ra-cha-nît-naí ?

คุณชอบกีฬาชนิดไหน ?

I like badminton.

chán-chorb-baed-min-ton.

ฉันชอบแบดมินตัน.

I can play badminton very well.

chán-lën-baed-min-ton-dai-dee-mak.

ฉันเล่นแบดมินตันได้ดีมาก.

Is there a badminton court here ?

theè-neè-mee-sä-nám-baed-min-ton-maí ?

ที่นี่มีสนามแบดมินตันไหม ?

Where's the nearest golf-course ?

sä-nám-kôrf-theè-klai-theè-sut-yöo-theè-naí ?

สนามกอล์ฟที่ใกล้ที่สุดอยู่ที่ไหน ?

Where are the tennis courts ?

sä-nám-then-nit-yöo-theè-naí ?

สนามเทนนิสอยู่ที่ไหน ?

What's the admission charge ?

sia-khà-khaò-thaò-rai ?

เสียค่าเข้าเท่าไร ?

What's the charge per hour/day/round ?

khà-lèn-chua-mong-la/wan-la/rorb-la/thaò-rai?

ค่าเล่น ชั่วโมงละ/วันละ/รอบละ เท่าไร ?

I would like to swim.

chán-yäk-waì-nâm.

ฉันอยากว่ายน้ำ.

Is there a swimming pool near here ?

mee-sa-waì-nâm-yöo-klai-klai-bàng-maí ?

มีสระว่ายน้ำอยู่ใกล้ ๆ บ้างไหม ?

Is it open air or indoor ?

yöo-nork-roé-nai-a-khan ?

อยู่นอกหรือในอาคาร ?

Can we go out fishing ?

rao-pai-tok-pla-kan-dee-maí ?

เราไปตกปลากันดีไหม ?

I'd like to see boxing match.

chán yä̲k-doo-muai.

ฉันอยากดูมวย.

Photographing

May I have these films developed ?

chán-tong-kan-lâng-feem-nêe ?

ฉันต้องการล้างฟิล์มนี้.

Please give me one print of this.

chuaì-at-haì-yăng-la-phàrb.

ช่วยอัดให้อย่างละภาพ.

I'd like to have this camera repaired.

chán-toȓng-kan-soȓm-kloȓng-thaï-roòp-nêe.

ฉันต้องการซ่อมกล้องถ่ายรูปนี้.

How long will it take you ?

khun-ja-chaì-we-la-nan-thaò-rai ?

คุณจะใช้เวลานานเท่าไร ?

How much do have I to pay ?

chán-ja-toȓng-sia-ngen-thaò-rai ?

ฉันจะต้องเสียเงินเท่าไร ?

Do you sell colour film ?

mee-feem-see-khaí-maí ?

มีฟิล์มสีขายไหม ?

I want a roll of film.

chán-toȓng-kan-feem-noëng-mûan.

ฉันต้องการฟิล์มหนึ่งม้วน.

How much is it ?

thaò-rai ?

เท่าไหร่ ?

Excuse me, could you direct me to the Grand palace ?

khoŕ-thòd-chuài-börk-thang-pai-phra-ba-rom-ma-há-rat-cha-wang-häi-thee.

ขอโทษ ! ช่วยบอกทางไปพระบรมมหาราชวังให้ที.

How can I get to the museum ?

chán-ja-pai-phi-phît-tha-phun-daì-yäng-rai ?

ฉันจะไปพิพิธภัณฑ์ได้อย่างไร ?

Go straight. Keep going straight.

dern-trong-pai.

เดินตรงไป.

Follow this...street.

dern-pai-tam-thä-nón-nêe.

เดินไปตามถนนนี้.

Is it the way to the temple of Emerald Buddha ?

thang-nêe-pai-wat-phra-kaèw-chaì-maí ?

ทางนี้ไปวัดพระแก้วใช่ไหม ?

Which street goes to the zoo ?

tha-nón-naí-pai-suán-sät ?

ถนนไหนไปสวนสัตว์ ?

Where does this street go ?

tha-nón-nêe-pai-naí ?

ถนนนี้ไปไหน ?

How far is the zoo from here ?

suán-sät-yöo-klai-jak-nêe-thaò-rai ?

สวนสัตว์อยู่ไกลจากนี้เท่าไร ?

It's fifteen minutes' walk.

dern-sib-hà-na-thee.

เดินสิบห้านาที.

It's ten minutes' drive.

khoèn-rôt-pai-sib-na-thee.

ขึ้นรถไปสิบนาที.

I'm lost.
chán-pai-mai-thöok.
ฉันไปไม่ถูก.

Walk on until you reach the cornor of the street.
dern-tör-pai-jon-thoéng-mum-thä-nón.
เดินต่อไปจนถึงมุมถนน.

Turn to the right.
liâw-khwá.
เลี้ยวขวา.

Turn left.
liâw-sâi.
เลี้ยวซ้าย.

Where is the shopping area ?
yàn-sôe-khoŕng-yöo-theè-nái ?
ย่านซื้อของอยู่ที่ไหน ?

You should take a taxi.
khun-khuan-pai-rot-rab-jàng.
คุณควรไปรถรับจ้าง.

Can I take a bus ?
pai-rot-pra-jam-thang-daì-maí ?
ไปรถประจำทางได้ไหม ?

Which bus must I take ?
toȑng-pai-khan-naí ?
ต้องไปคันไหน?

How long it will take me ?

tor̲ng-châi-we̲-la̲-na̲n-thaò-rai ?

ต้องใช้เวลานานเท่าไร ?

The bus will be very crowded.

rot-pra-jam-thang-ja-naèn-màk̲.

รถประจำทางจะแน่นมาก.

How can I go to the Marble Temple ?

chán-ja-pai-wat-ben-ja-daì-ya̲ng-rai ?

ฉันจะไปวัดเบญจได้อย่างไร ?

Cross the street.

de̲rn-khà̲m-tha-non-pai.

เดินข้ามถนนไป.

It's on your right/left.

yöo-thang-khwá-mo̲e̲/sâi-mo̲e̲.

อยู่ทางขวามือ/ซ้ายมือ.

It's infront of you.

yöo-kha̲ng-nà̲-khun.

อยู่ข้างหน้าคุณ.

hire,	chaò	เช่า,
hiring	kan-chaò	การเช่า
car	rôt	รถ

I'd like to hire a car, please.
chán-yăk-chaò-rôt.
ฉันอยากเช่ารถ.

I want to use the car during the day.
chán-toŕng-kan-châi-rôt-we-la-klang-wan.
ฉันต้องการใช้รถเวลากลางวัน.

I want the car at ten o'clock.
chán-toŕng-kan-rot-we-la-sib-mong.
ฉันต้องการรถเวลาสิบโมง.

How many hours a day ?
wan-la-kee-chuà-mong ?
วันละกี่ชั่วโมง ?

About five hours a day.
wan-la-hà-chuà-mong.
วันละ 5 ชั่วโมง.

How much is it for a day ?
khit-wan-la-thaò-rai ?
คิดวันละเท่าไร ?

How much is it per hour ?
khit-chuà-mong-la-thaò-rai ?
คิดชั่วโมงละเท่าไร ?

I want to hire a car for a week.

chán-torǹg-kan-chaò-rôt-sab-da-noëng.

ฉันต้องการเช่ารถสัปดาห์หนึ่ง.

How much does it cost ?

Khit-thaò-rai ?

คิดเท่าไร ?

Can I pay you per day ?

jai-pen-rai-ẇan-daì-maí ?

จ่ายเป็นรายวันได้ไหม ?

Is there a driver ?

mee-khon-khäb-maí ?

มีคนขับไหม ?

Can I see the car, please ?

khoŕ-doo-rôt-daì-maí ?

ขอดูรถได้ไหม ?

Drive slowly.

khab-châ-châ.

ขับช้า ๆ

Don't drive so fast.

yä-khäb-rew.

อย่าขับเร็ว.

Please stop here a minute.

yüd-theè-neè-sak-khroò.

หยุดที่นี่สักครู่.

Drive along that street.

khab-pai-ta̲m-thä-nón-nân.

ขับไปตามถนนนั้น.

Drive straight on.

khab-trong-pai.

ขับตรงไป.

Back to the hotel.

kläb-ro̲ng-ra̲e̲m.

กลับโรงแรม.

I want to use the car again on Sunday.

chán-tõ̲rng-ka̲n-chaî-rôt-ëek-nai-wan-a̲-thît.

ฉันต้องการใช้รถอีกในวันอาทิตย์.

Please give me a package of cigarettes.
a box of matches.

khor̲-bü-ree-noëng-song.

khor̲-mâi-kheet-klörng-no̲ëng.

ขอบุหรี่หนึ่งซอง.

ขอไม้ขีดกล่องหนึ่ง.

How much is this shirt ?

so̲eà-chêrt-tua-nêe-ra̲-kha̲-thaò-rai ?

เสื้อเชิ้ตตัวนี้ราคาเท่าไร ?

It's expensive.

pha̲eng-pai.

แพงไป.

Can you make it cheaper ?

lôd-ra̲-kha̲-dai̲-maí ?

ลดราคาได้ไหม ?

I want it cheaper.

chán-ya̲k-dai-ra̲-kha̲-thöok-kwa̲-nêe.·nêe.

ฉันอยากได้ราคาถูกกว่านี้.

It's too big / small

yäi-pai /lêk-pai

ใหญ่ไป / เล็กไป

I want a larger one/a smaller one.

chán-tor-kan-tua-yäi/lek/-kwä-nêe.

ฉันต้องการตัวใหญ่/เล็ก/กว่านี้.

Do you have a better one ?

mee-dee-kwä-tua-nêe-maí ?

มีดีกว่าตัวนี้ไหม ?

I don't like that one.

chán-maì-chorb-tua-nân;

ฉันไม่ชอบตัวนั้น.

Give me this one.

khoř-tua-nêe.

ขอตัวนี้.

How much is it all together ?

ruam-thâng-möd-pen-thaò-rai ?

รวมทั้งหมดเป็นเท่าไร ?

Can I pay in dollar/in travelling chaque.

jai-pen-don-la/pen-chek-dern-tang/-daì-maí ?

จ่ายเป็นดอลล่าร์/เป็นเช็คเดินทาง/ได้ไหม ?

Can you send it to my room at the hotel ?

Söng-pai-theè-hòng-phak-theè-rong-raem-daì-maí ?

ส่งไปที่ห้องพักที่โรงแรมได้ไหม ?

Please give me the charge/the receipt.

khoŕ-ngern-thorn/bai-râb-ngern.

ขอเงินทอน/ใบรับเงิน.

Illness

illness	khwa̲m-jëb-puai	ความเจ็บป่วย

I'm not well.
chán-maì-sä-bai.
ฉันไม่สบาย.

I feel very ill.
chán-maì-sä-bai-ma̲k.
ฉันไม่สบายมาก.

I feel dizzy.
chán-wia̲n-seé-sä.
ฉันเวียนศีรษะ.

I feel giddy.
chán-khloe̲n-saĭ.
ฉันคลื่นไส้.

I have a headache

- stomachache
- fever
- a cough.

chán-puad-seé-sä.

- puäd-thôrng
- pen-khai.
- ai

ฉันปวดศีรษะ

- ปวดท้อง
- เป็นไข้
- ไอ

I'm feeling week.

chán-örn-phlia.

ฉันอ่อนเพลีย.

It happened yesterday.

pen-moea-wan-nêe.

เป็นเมื่อวานนี้.

It has not happened before.

mai-khoei-pen-ma-körn.

ไม่เคยเป็นมาก่อน.

It gets worse.

pen-mak-khoèn.

เป็นมากขึ้น.

I did not eat anything bad.
chán-maì-daì-kin-a-rai-maì-dee.
ฉันไม่ได้กินอะไรไม่ดี.

Did you sleep well last night ?
moeà-khoen-norn-läb-maí ?
เมื่อคืนนอนหลับไหม ?

No, I had a bad night.
chán-norn-maì-lab.
ฉันนอนไม่หลับ.

Keep yourself warm.
tham-tua-haì-ün.
ทำตัวให้อุ่น.

stay still.
yöo-choeí-choeí.
อยู่เฉย ๆ

Rest well.
phak-haì-dee.
พักให้ดี.

How is your appetite ?
rab-pra-than-daì-maí ?
รับประทานได้ไหม ?

I can't eat anything.
chán-rab-pra-than-a-rai-maì-daì-loei.
ฉันรับประทานอะไรไม่ได้เลย.

Try to eat soft food.

pha-ya-yam-rab-pra-than-a-hán-örn-örn.

พยายามรับประทานอาหารอ่อน ๆ.

You must stay in bed.

khun-to̖rng-norn-phâk.

คุณต้องนอนพัก.

Try to sleep more.

pha-ya-yam-norn-hai̖-mak.

พยายามนอนให้มาก.

I'll give you medicine.

chán-ja-hai-ya-khun.

ฉันจะให้ยาคุณ.

Take it two at a time, every four hours.

rab-pra-than-khrang-la-so̒rng-met-thûk-sëe-chuà-mong.

รับประทานครั้งละ 2 เม็ด ทุก 4 ชั่วโมง.

What are your fees, doctor ?

mo̒r-khit-khà-ya-thaò-rai ?

หมอคิดค่ายาเท่าไร ?

I'll call you again.

chán-ja-ma-ëek.

ฉันจะมาอีก.

I feel much better.

chán-khòi-yang-chuà-khoen̖-mak.

ฉันค่อยยังชั่วขึ้นมาก.

Don't take a bath.

yä-äb-nâm.

อย่าอาบน้ำ.

Visiting

to visit	pai-yiàm	ไปเยี่ยม
visiting	ka̲n-yiàm	การเยี่ยม

May I call on you ?

chán-pai-há̲-khun-daì-maí ?

ฉันไปหาคุณได้ไหม ?

Will you be at home on Sunday ?

wan-a̲-thit-nêe-khun-ja-yöo-bà̲n-maí ?

วันอาทิตย์นี้คุณจะอยู่บ้านไหม ?

At what time ?

këe-mong ?

กี่โมง ?

At what time will be convenient for you ?

këe-mong-khun-ja-sä-duäk.

กี่โมงคุณจะสะดวก ?

Would one o'clock be alright ?

bäi-mong-daì-maí ?

บ่ายโมงได้ไหม ?

Please come in.

chern-khàng-nai.

เชิญข้างใน.

Glad to see you.

yin-dee-theè-daì-phob-khun.

ยินดีที่ได้พบคุณ.

How are you ?

sä-bau-dee-roé ?

สบายดีหรือ ?

Please take a seat.

chern-nàng.

เชิญนั่ง.

What can I do for you ?

May I help you ?

chán-ja-chuaì-a-rai-daì-bàng ?

ฉันจะช่วยอะไรได้บ้าง ?

I just come to see you.

chán-ma-yìam-khun-thaò-nân.

ฉันมาเยี่ยมคุณเท่านั้น.

I enjoy seeing and talking with you.

chán-chòrb-theè-daì-phôb-lâe-khui-käb-khun.

ฉันชอบที่ได้พบและคุยกับคุณ.

I must go now.

I have to leave now.

chán-tòrng-klab-laèw.

ฉันต้องกลับแล้ว.

Why in a hurry ?

tham-mai-reèb-kläb-nâk ?

ทำไมรีบกลับนัก ?

I have an appointment at four o'clock.

chán-mee-nât-we-la-bai-sëe-mong.

ฉันมีนัดเวลาบ่าย 4 โมง.

Please come again sometime.

chern-ma-ëek.

เชิญมาอีก.

At the Laundry and Barber's shop

Barber's shop Hair dresser's	rân-tham-phom	ร้านทำผม
laundry	rân-sâk-reèt	ร้านซักรีด

Can you clean - this coat.
- this raincoat.
- this shirt
- this pair of trousers.

chán-tong-karn-sâk - soeà-nêe.
- soeà-fón.
- soeà-chêrt.
- kang-keng.

ฉันต้องการซัก - เสื้อนี้
- เสื้อฝน
- เสื้อเชิ้ต
- กางเกง

Please mend this dress.

chuai-sorm-soeà-kra-prong-chûd-nêe.

ช่วยซ่อมเสื้อกระโปรงชุดนี้.

When will it be ready ?

ja-sët-moeà-rai ?

จะเสร็จเมื่อไร ?

Is there - a hair dresser's shop
- a barber's shop.
around here ?

mee - râ̲n-täeng-phóm
- râ̲n-tät-phóm. tháe̲w-nêe-bà̲ng-mai ?

มี มีร้านแต่งผม
ร้านตัดผม แถวนี้บ้างไหม ?

Is there a beauty salon in the Hotel ?

mee-râ̲n-sé̲rm-suaí-nai-ro̲ng-rae̲m-maí ?

มีร้านเสริมสวยในโรงแรมไหม ?

I would like to go to a hair dresser's.

chán-yă̲k-pai-râ̲n-tham-phóm.

ฉันอยากไปร้านทำผม.

I want my hair washed and set.

chán-tò̲rng-ka̲n-sä-lâe-tham-phóm.

ฉันต้องการสระและทำผม.

Can I make an appointment on Sunday ?

chán-nât-wan-a̲-thit-we̲-la̲-dai-kò̲r-daì ?

ฉันนัดวันอาทิตย์เวลาใดก็ได้.

I want my hair dyed.

chán-tò̲rng-ka̲n-yô̲rm-phóm.

ฉันต้องการย้อมผม.

I would like my hair cut/waved.

chán-tò̲rng-ka̲n-tat-phóm-/dät-phóm.

ฉันต้องการตัดผม/ดัดผม.

What kind of solution do you now have ?

theè-nêe-châi-nâm-ya̲-a-rai ?

ที่นี่ใช้น้ำยาอะไร ?

Is it good ?

dee-maí ?

ดีไหม ?

Does it make the curl last long ?

tham-haì-phóm-yǐk-thon-mái ?

ทำให้ผมหยิกทนไหม ?

Do you sell hair-spray ?

mee-sä-pre̱-khäi-maí ?

มีสเปรย์ขายไหม ?

What hair-style will suit me ?

phóm-bäe̱b-naí-mör-kab-chán ?

ผมแบบไหนเหมาะกับฉัน ?

Do you give a facial treatment here ?

theè-nêe-râb-taëng-nà̱-maí ?

ที่นี่รับแต่งหน้าไหม ?

Don't cut it too short.

yä̱-tat-sàn-nâk.

อย่าตัดสั้นนัก.

I want some cleansing cream.

chán-tò̱rng-ka̱n-khreem-lâ̱ng-nâ̱.

ฉันต้องการครีมล้างหน้า.

I also need some skin food.

chán-tò̱rng-ka̱n-nâm-ya̱-bam-rung-phiw-duaì.

ฉันต้องการน้ำยาบำรุงผิวด้วย.

I should like a menicure/pedicre.

chán-to̲rng-ka̲n-tham-lêb-mo̲e̲/lêb-thâo.

ฉันต้องการทำเล็บมือ/เล็บเท้า.

I like pink shade.

chán-cho̲r̲b-seé-chom-phoo.

ฉันชอบสีชมพู.

How much for all ?

thâng-möd-thaò-rai ?

ทั้งหมดเท่าไร ?

I would like to go to the barber's shop.

chán-ya̲k-pai-rá̲n-tät-phóm.

ฉันอยากไปร้านตัดผม.

I want my hair cut.

chán-ya̲k-tät-phóm.

ฉันอยากตัดผม.

Do I have to wait long ?

to̲r̲ng-khoi-na̲n-mai ?

ต้องคอยนานไหม ?

How do you like your hair cut ?

khun-cho̲r̲b-hai-tät-phóm-ya̲ng-rai ?

คุณชอบให้ตัดผมอย่างไร ?

Just trim it.

lem-thaò-nân.

เล็มเท่านั้น.

I like it cut like this.

tat-tam-baeb-nêe.

ตัดตามแบบนี้.

Short at the sides.

tat-khàng-haì-sàn.

ตัดข้างให้สั้น.

Not to short on the top.

khàng-bon-maì-toìng-sàn-nâk.

ข้างบนไม่ต้องสั้นนัก.

I want to thin out my hair.

chán-toìng-kan-soi-phóm.

ฉันต้องการซอยผม.

Wash my hair too.

sä-phóm-haì-duaì.

สระผมให้ด้วย.

I want a shampoo.

sä-duai-chaem-phoo.

สระด้วยแชมพู.

Apply a little pomade.

säi-nâm-man-nît-nöi.

ใส่น้ำมันนิดหน่อย.

I want a shave.

chán-toìng-kan-kon-nüad.

ฉันต้องการโกนหนวด.

How much do have I to pay ?

chán-ja-tor̲ng-jai-ngern-thao-rai ?

ฉันจะต้องจ่ายเงินเท่าไร ?

At the Bank

Bank thâ-na-kan ธนาคาร

Is there a bank around here ?
thaéw-nêe-mee-thâ-na-kan-maí ?
แถวนี้มีธนาคารไหม ?

I'd like to change my money.
chán-torng-kan-laèk-ngern.
ฉันต้องการแลกเงิน.

Please change the money into Thai money.
laèk-ngern-nêe-pen-ngern-thai.
แลกเงินนี้เป็นเงินไทย.

Please cash the cheque.
khoŕ-bërk-ngern-söd.
ขอเบิกเงินสด.

Please give me note/small changes.
khór-pen-tha-na-bat/pet-ngern-yoì.
ขอเป็นธนบัตร/เป็นเงินย่อย.

Where can I cash my traveller's cheque ?
chán-ja-laèk-check-dern-thang-dai-theè-naí ?
ฉันจะแลกเช็คเดินทางได้ที่ไหน ?

Where is the foreign exchange department ?
pha-näek-laèk-ngern-tang-pra-thèd-yöo-theè-naí ?
แผนกแลกเงินต่างประเทศอยู่ที่ไหน ?

What's the rate of exchange today ?
at-tra-laèk-pliǐan-wan-nêe-pen-thaò-rai. ?
อัตราแลกเปลี่ยนวันนี้เป็นเท่าไร ?

Where is the money changer ?
theè-laèk-ngern-yöo-theè-naí ?
ที่แลกเงินอยู่ที่ไหน ?

I'd like to sell my dollar.
chán-ja-khaǐ-ngern-don-là.
ฉันจะขายเงินดอลล่าร์.

I'd like to buy some pounds.
chán-yak-sôe-ngern-porn.
ฉันอยากซื้อเงินปอนด์.

What's rate of commission do you charge ?
khun-khît-khà-laèk-thaò-rai ?
คุณคิดค่าแลกเท่าไร ?

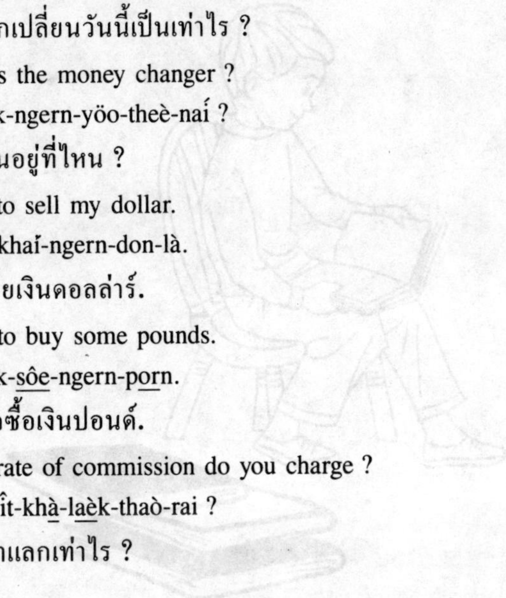

At the Book Store

book-store	rân-khaí-nâng-soé	ร้านขายหนังสือ
book	náng-soé	หนังสือ
stationery	rán-khaí-khroeàng-khián	ร้านขายเครื่องเขียน
newspaper	náng-soé-phim	หนังสือพิมพ์
dictionary	phot-ja-na-nu-krom	พจนานุกรม
novel	na-wa-ni-yai	นวนิยาย

ink	nâm-möek	น้ำหมึก
pencil	din-soŕ	ดินสอ
pen	päk-ka	ปากกา
fountain pen	päk-ka-möek-soem	ปากกาหมึกซึม
evelope	sorng-jöt-maí	ซองจดหมาย

weekly magazine.
náng-soé-rai-sab-da.
หนังสือรายสัปดาห์.

writing paper.
kra-dät-khián-náng-soé.
กระดาษเขียนหนังสือ.

wrapping paper.
kra-dät-hör-khoŕng.
กระดาษห่อของ.

carbon paper.
kra-dät-ad-sám-nao.
กระดาษอัดสำเนา.

blotting paper.
kra-dät-sab.
กระดาษซับ.

Where is your luggage/hand-bag ?
kra-paó-khorńg-khun-yöo-theè-naí ?
กระเป๋าของคุณอยู่ที่ไหน ?

What have you got in the bag ?
mee-a-rai-yöo-nai-kra-paó ?
มีอะไรอยู่ในกระเป๋า ?

Nothing except personal effects.
maì-mee-a-rai-noȓk-jäk-khorńg-châi-suän-tua.
ไม่มีอะไรนอกจากของใช้ส่วนตัว.

Please open your bag.
pröd-për d-kra-paó-khorńg-khun.
โปรดเปิดกระเป๋าของคุณ.

Is there anything to declare ?
mee-a-rai-toȓng-jaèng-maí ?
มีอะไรต้องแจ้งไหม ?

No, nothing.
maì-mee.
ไม่มี.

Are all these things yours ?
khorńg-thâng-möd-nêe-pen-khorńg-khun-roé ?
ของทั้งหมดนี้เป็นของคุณหรือ ?

I have examined them.
chán-trüat-lâew.
ฉันตรวจแล้ว.

How much money do you have with you ?
khun-mee-ngern-ma-thaò-rai ?
คุณมีเงินมาเท่าไร ?

How long do you intend to stay ?
khun-ja-yöo-nan-thaò-rai ?
คุณจะอยู่นานเท่าไร ?

What time is it now ?
kee-mong-lâew ?
กี่โมงแล้ว ?

Where is the bank ?
tha-na-khan-yöo-naí ?
ธนาคารอยู่ไหน ?

I want to change my money.
chán-toǹg-kan-laèk-ngern.
ฉันต้องการแลกเงิน.

Call me a porter.
riàk-khon-khón-khoŕng-hai-thee.
เรียกคนขนของให้ที.

Call me a taxi.
riak-rôt-rab-jang-hai-duài.
เรียกรถรับจ้างให้ด้วย.

Where can I get a taxi ?
chán-ja-há-rôt-râb-jàng-daì-theè-naí ?
ฉันจะหารถรับจ้างได้ที่ไหน ?

Go to the Hotel, please.
pai-theè-rong-raem.
ไปที่โรงแรม
Go slowler, please.
khäb-châ-châ-noi̇̈.
ขับช้า ๆ หน่อย.
Stop here, please.
yud-theè-nèe.
หยุดที่นี่.
How much is it ?
khà-rôt-thaò-rai ?
ค่ารถเท่าไร ?
Keep the change.
këb-ngern-thorn-wâi.
เก็บเงินทอนไว้.

In our country, we do not tip anyone. However, you can do what you get used to, and you will be appreciated.

At the Hotel

You are now checking in at your hotel. At the front desk of any good hotel, the clerk can speak English. Most hotels in Bangkok are quite good and their service is rather friendly. Thus, you will enjoy your stay with in.

Checking in

I have a reservation.
chán-jorng-hòrng-wâi-laêw.
ฉันจองห้องไว้แล้ว.

I haven't a reservation.
chán-yang-maì-daì-jorng-hòrng.
ฉันยังไม่ได้จองห้อง.

How long would you like to stay ?
khun-ja-yöo-nan-thaò-rai ?
คุณจะอยู่นานเท่าไร ?

About ten days.
prä-man-sïb-wan.
ประมาณ 10 วัน.

A single or a double room sir ?
tòrng-kan-hòrng-dïaw-roé-hòrng-khoò ?
ต้องการห้องเดี่ยวหรือห้องคู่ ?

A single room with bath.
hòrng-dïaw-mee-hòrng-nâm.
ห้องเดี่ยวมีห้องน้ำ.

Feliz Navidad y Próspero Añ
Battle of Hastings 1066
HAPPINESS
CHRISTMA
POSTES POSTAGE
MERRY CHRISTMAS AND A HAPPY NEW YEAR
REPUBLIQUE FRANÇAISE
VIIIe CENTENAIRE
CATHEDRALE DE SENS
FROHE WEIHNA
Christmas
JOYEUX NOËL ET BONNE ANNÉE

ประเทศไทย THAILAND
POSTAGE
COVERED BOWLS, BENCHARONG WARE
2.75 บาท BAHT
HELVETIA 20
1815-1965 VALAIS NEUCHÂTEL GENÈVE
FRIEDEN
PAX
TERRA
POSTE VATICANE L.20
God Jul och Gott Nytt År
Prettige Kerstdagen en Gelukkig Nieuwjaar

How much does it cost ?
khà-chaò-wan-la-thaò-rai ?
ค่าเช่าวันละเท่าไร ?
Can I see the room first.
khoŕ-doo-hor̀ng-kor̈n.
ขอดูห้องก่อน.
It's on the fourth floor.
hor̀ng-yöo-chân-sëe.
ห้องอยู่ชั้น 4.
Do you have a better room ?
mee-hor̀ng-dee-kwä-nêe-maí ?
มีห้องดีกว่านี้ไหม ?
Do you have an inexpensive room ?
mee-hor̀ng-ra-kha-thöok-kwä-nêe-maí ?
มีห้องราคาถูกกว่านี้ไหม ?
I like quiet room.
chán-chorb-hor̀ng-ngiàb-ngiàb.
ฉันชอบห้องเงียบ ๆ.
All right, I'll take this room.
tök-long-chán-ao-hor̀ng-nèe.
ตกลงฉันเอาห้องนี้.
Where can I exchange the money ?
chán-ja-laèk-ngern-daì-theè-naí ?
ฉันจะแลกเงินได้ที่ไหน ?

What is the rate of exchange for today ?

ăt-tra-laèk-plïan-wan-nêe-thaò-rai ?

อัตราแลกเปลี่ยนวันนี้เท่าไร ?

Where is the dining room ?

horng-râb-pra-than-a-hán-yöo-theè-naí ?

ห้องรับประทานอาหารอยู่ที่ไหน ?

What time is breakfast/lunch/dinner ?

a-hán-châo

a-hán-klang-wan we-la-a-rai ?

a-hán-yen.

อาหารเช้า/อาหารกลางวัน/อาหารเย็น เวลาอะไร ?

Can I have breakfast/tea/coffee in my room, please ?

khoŕ-a-hán-châo/cha/ka-fae/-nai-horng.

ขออาหารเช้า/ชา/กาแฟ ในห้อง.

Please bring more tea.

khoŕ-nâm-cha-ëek.

ขอนำชาอีก.

The room is too cold/warm.

horng-yen/rôrn-pai.

ห้องเย็น/ร้อนไป.

Will you mail this ?

chuaì-söng-thang-prai-sä-nee-hài-thee.

ช่วยส่งทางไปรษณีย์ให้ที.

I feel bad.
chán-mai-sa-bai.
ฉันไม่สบาย.

He is sick.
khaó-maì-sä-bai.
เขาไม่สบาย.

Is there a doctor near here ?
mee-moŕ-yöo-klaì-klaì-maí ?
มีหมออยู่ใกล้ ๆ ไหม ?

Will you call a doctor ?
chuaì-riàk-moŕ-haì-thee ?
ช่วยเรียกหมอให้ที.

The air-condition/fan/light/toilet/does not work.
khoèang-prab-a-kät/phad-lom/fai-fâ/hoŕng-nâm/siá.
เครื่องปรับอากาศ/พัดลม/ไฟฟ้า/ห้องน้ำ/เสีย.

There's no hot water.
maì-mee-nâm-rôrn.
ไม่มีน้ำร้อน.

I've lost my key/watch.
chán-tham-kun-jae/na-rî-ka/haí.
ฉันทำกุญแจ/นาฬิกา/หาย.

I've left my key in my room.
chán-loem-kun-jae-wai-nai-hoŕng.
ฉันลืมกุญแจไว้ในห้อง.

Please bring me a towel/a pillow.
khoŕ-phà-hŏm/moŕn.
ขอผ้าห่ม/หมอน.

Can you call me number..........?
chuaì-tŏr-maí-lèk..........
ช่วยต่อหมายเลข..........

Did any one call me ?
me-khrai-tho-ra-säb-thoéng-chán-bàng-maí ?
มีใครโทรศัพท์ถึงฉันบ้างไหม ?

There is a telephone call for you.
mee-tho-ra-säb-thoéng-khun.
มีโทรศัพท์ถึงคุณ.

I'll call him back.
chán-ja-tho-kläb-ha-khaó.
ฉันจะโทรกลับหาเขา

Have you any stamps ?
mee-sä-team-maí ?
มีแสตมป์ไหม ?

Are there any messages for me ?
mee-jöd-maí-thoèng-chán-maí ?
มีจดหมายถึงฉันไหม ?

I'm going out.
chán-ja-örk-pai-khàng-noŕk.
ฉันจะออกไปข้างนอก.

I'll be back in the afternoon.

chán-ja-klab-ma-torn-baï.

ฉันจะกลับมาตอนบ่าย.

Please get me a taxi.

chuaì-riàk-rôt-taêk-seè-haì-duaì.

ช่วยเรียกรถแท็กซี่ให้ด้วย.

Checking out

I'm leaving early tomorrow.

chán-ja-pai-phrung-nêe-châo.

ฉันจะไปพรุ่งนี้เช้า.

Please have my bill ready.

khit-ngern-haì-set-duài.

คิดเงินให้เสร็จด้วย.

We'll be checking out this evening.

rao-ja-pai-yen-wan-nêe.

เราจะไปเย็นวันนี้.

I must leave now.

chán-ja-toìng-pai-diáw-nêe.

ฉันจะต้องไปเดี๋ยวนี้.

Does this include everything ?

khit-möd-tuk-yang-laêw-roé?

คิดหมดทุกอย่างแล้วหรือ ?

Please give me my bill.
khoŕ-bai-râb-ngern.

ขอใบรับเงิน.

Do you take traveller's cheque ?
khun-râb-chêk-dern-tang-maí ?

คุณรับเช็คเดินทางไหม ?

Make the bills separately.
tham-bil-yaèk-duaì.

ทำบิลแยกด้วย.

Would you bring down our beggage ?
chuaì-yok-kra-paó-long-pai-duaì.

ช่วยยกกระเป๋าลงไปด้วย.

We're in a great hurry.
rao-kam-lang-reeb.

เรากำลังรีบ.

Can you get me a taxi.
riak-rôt-tâek-seè-haì-duaì.

เรียกรถแท็กซี่ให้ด้วย.

Here is my home address.
neè-koe-tam-bon-theè-yöo-khoŕng-chán.

นี่คือตำบลที่อยู่ของฉัน.

It's a very enjoyable stay.
phak-theè-neè-dee-mak.

พักที่นี่ดีมาก.

I hope we will come again sometime.

rao-khong-ja-daì-ma-theè-neè-ëek.
เราคงจะได้มาที่นี่อีก.

Where do you come from ?

khun-ma-jäk-nai ?

คุณมาจากไหน ?

Do you like it here ?

khun-chorb-theè-neè-maí ?

คุณชอบที่นี่ไหม ?

Where are you staying ?

khun-phâk-yöo-theè-naí ?

คุณพักอยู่ที่ไหน ?

When did you arrive in Bangkok ?

khun-ma-thoéng-krung-thèp-moeà-rai ?

คุณมาถึงกรุงเทพฯเมื่อไร ?

Do you understand English ?

khun-khaò-jai-pha-sá-ang-krït-maí ?

คุณเข้าใจภาษาอังกฤษไหม ?

Let's speak English.

phoòd-pha-sá-ang-krit-kan-thër.

พูดภาษาอังกฤษกันเถอะ.

Please speak slowly.

pröd-phoòd-châ-châ.

โปรดพูดช้า ๆ .

Pardon me, I can't follow you.

khoŕ-thòd-chán-fang-mai-rôo-roèang.

ขอโทษฉันฟังไม่รู้เรื่อง.

I have something to tell you.

chán-mee-roèang-ja-börk-khun.

ฉันมีเรื่องจะบอกคุณ.

Do you want this ?

khun-tòrng-kan-sïng-nêe-maí ?

คุณต้องการสิ่งนี้ไหม ?

I don't think so.

chán-khît-wà-maì.

ฉันคิดว่าไม่.

I hope so.

chán-koȑ-khit-wà-yăng-nân.

ฉันก็คิดว่าอย่างนั้น.

I believe so.

chán-choeà-wà-yăng-nân.

ฉันเชื่อว่าอย่างนั้น.

I believe not.

chán-mai-choeà-wà-j̈a-pen-yăng-nân.

ฉันไม่เชื่อว่าเป็นอย่างนั้น.

Would you like to go out ?

khun-ja-örk-pai-khàng-noȑk-maí ?

คุณจะออกไปข้างนอกไหม ?

Where are you going ?

khun-ja-pai-naí ?

คุณจะไปไหน ?

Where have you been ?

khun-pai-naí-ma ?

คุณไปไหนมา ?

Are you ready to go ?

khun-phrôrm-thèe-ja-pai-roé-yang ?

คุณพร้อมที่จะไปหรือยัง ?

I'm busy.

chán-kam-lang-yùng.

ฉันกำลังยุ่ง.

I'm tired.

chán-noëai.

ฉันเหนื่อย.

Just a moment.

Wait a moment.

khoi-säk-khroò.

คอยสักครู่.

Wait here.

khoi-yöo-theè-neè.

คอยอยู่ที่นี่.

Wait for me.

khoi-chán-körn.

คอยฉันก่อน.

Tell him to wait.

börk-hai-khaó-khoi.

บอกให้เขาคอย.

What do you mean ?

What does it mean ?

maí-kwam-wà-yäng-rai ?

หมายความว่าอย่างไร ?

I can't follow you.

chán-fang-mai-than.

ฉันฟังไม่ทัน.

Don't speak so fast.

yä-phoòd-rew-nâk.

อย่าพูดเร็วนัก.

Can you speak - English ?

- Thai ?

khun-phoòd-pha-sá-/ang-krit/thai/daì-maí ?

คุณพูดภาษา อังกฤษ / ไทย ได้ไหม ?

I can speak a little.

phoòd-daí-nît-nöi.

พูดได้นิดหน่อย.

Is that so ?

yäng-nân-roé ?

อย่างนั้นหรือ ?

What's the matter ?

roèang-a-rai-kan ?

เรื่องอะไรกัน ?

What's the matter with you ?

khun-pen-a-rai ?

คุณเป็นอะไร ?

Nothing's the matter ?

mai-mee-roèang-a-rai ?

ไม่มีเรื่องอะไร ?

What language do you speak ?

khun-phoòd-pha-sá-a-rai ?

คุณพูดภาษาอะไร ?

Where is/the British Embassy ?
Post office ?

sä-thán-thoòt-ang-krit/
theè-tham-kan-prai-sä-nee. yöo-theè-naí ?

สถานทูตอังกฤษ
ที่ทำการไปรษณีย์. อยู่ที่ไหน ?

Where is/the police station ?
the police box ?

sa-thá-nee-tam-ruäd/ yöo-theè-naí ?
porm-tam-ruäd.

สถานีตำรวจ/
ป้อมตำรวจ. อยู่ที่ไหน ?

What is your name ?

khun-choè-a-rai ?

คุณชื่ออะไร ?

Have you got a phone ?

khun-mee-tho-râ-säp-maí ?

คุณมีโทรศัพท์ไหม ?

What is your phone number ?

lèk-maí-tho-râ-sap-khoŕng-khun-thaò-rai ?

เลขหมายโทรศัพท์ของคุณเท่าไร ?

Where do you live ?

khun-yöo-theè-naí ?

คุณอยู่ที่ไหน ?

I stay at Silom Hotel.

chán-yöo-rong-raem-seé-lom.

ฉันอยู่ที่โรงแรมสีลม.

What's the weather going to be like......... ?

- today ?
- tomorrow ?
- this evening ?
- to night ?

a-kät-ja-pen-yäng-rai....

- wan-nêe.
- phrùng-nêe.
- yen-nêe.
- khoen-nêe.

อากาศจะเป็นอย่างไร...

- วันนี้ ?
- พรุ่งนี้ ?
- เย็นนี้ ?
- คืนนี้ ?

Is it going to rain ?
- to be sunny ?
- to be cold ?
- to be hot ?

fón-kam-lang-ja-tök
däed-kam-lang-ja-örk ?
a-kät-kam-lang-ja-yen
a-kät-kam-lang-ja-rôrn

roé ?

ฝนกำลังจะตก
แดดกำลังจะออก
อากาศจะเย็น
อากาศจะร้อน

หรือ ?

Is the weather going to change ?
a-kat-kam-lang-ja-plïan-roé ?
อากาศกำลังจะเปลี่ยนหรือ ?